The
Small
Talk
HANDBOOK

The
Small
Talk
HANDBOOK

EASY INSTRUCTIONS ON HOW TO MAKE SMALL TALK IN ANY SITUATION

MELISSA WADSWORTH

Avon, Massachusetts

Published by
Adams Media, a division of F+W Media, Inc.
57 Littlefield Street, Avon, MA 02322. U.S.A.
www.adamsmedia.com

ISBN 10: 1-4405-5016-6
ISBN 13: 978-1-4405-5016-4
eISBN 10: 1-4405-5017-4
eISBN 13: 978-1-4405-5017-1

Printed in the United States of America.

10   9   8   7   6   5   4   3   2   1

Library of Congress Cataloging-in-Publication Data
Wadsworth, Melissa.
The small talk handbook / Melissa Wadsworth.
p. cm.
Rev. ed. of: Small talk savvy.
ISBN 978-1-4405-5016-4 (pbk.) – ISBN 1-4405-5016-6 (pbk.) – ISBN 978-1-4405-5017-1
(ebook) – ISBN 1-4405-5017-4 (ebook)
1. Conversation. 2. Oral communication. I. Wadsworth, Melissa. Small talk savvy. II. Title.
BJ2121.W23 2012
395.5'9–dc23
2012014765

Originally published under the title *Small Talk Savvy* by Melissa Wadsworth; copyright
© 2005 by F+W Media, Inc., ISBN 10: 1-59337-570-0, ISBN 13: 978-1-59337-570-6.

This publication is designed to provide accurate and authoritative information with regard
to the subject matter covered. It is sold with the understanding that the publisher is not
engaged in rendering legal, accounting, or other professional advice. If legal advice or other
expert assistance is required, the services of a competent professional person should be
sought.
    —From a *Declaration of Principles* jointly adopted by a Committee of the American Bar
Association and a Committee of Publishers and Associations

Many of the designations used by manufacturers and sellers to distinguish their product
are claimed as trademarks. Where those designations appear in this book and Adams Media
was aware of a trademark claim, the designations have been printed with initial capital
letters.

This book is available at quantity discounts for bulk purchases.
For information, please call 1-800-289-0963.

Contents

Acknowledgments • 9

Introduction • 11

1 Small Talk Starter Kit • 15

2 Talking It Up with Body Language • 27

3 Savvy Socializing • 45

4 Social Ease on the Dating Scene • 61

5 Everyday Mingling • 77

6 Nourishing Small Talk: Home Entertaining and Business Meals • 91

7 Small Talk Muscle in the Workplace • 105

8 Interaction Strategies Outside the Office • 119

9 Taking Stock of Your Small Talk Skills • 135

Appendix • 149

Index • 153

Acknowledgments

This was truly a collaborative effort. I was fortunate in the writing of this book to have a wealth of friendships and their diverse array of professional experiences that I could draw upon. Thank you to all my family and friends (and parents of friends), who contributed their social and business stories and bits of communication wisdom. I enjoyed hearing many of the stories for the first time, and was grateful to be able to share them. Once again experiencing the full measure of these connections, especially the deep generosity that flowed my way, has been a gift itself.

Thank you to my writing buddy, Patti, who provided such helpful input chapter by chapter. Her comments were right on and, I think, really helped me to create a book that is consistently enjoyable to read.

Much love and gratitude go to my husband, Tracy, my greatest supporter, who has always provided a safe and giving atmosphere in which to explore and grow my writing endeavors.

I thank my agent, Pamela Brodowsky, for having faith in my writing skills. That confidence manifested in this opportunity, for which I am very happy to have been presented.

Finally, thank you to book editor Danielle Chiotti for the chance to plunge into a project that has been a wonderful learning experience—reminding me how important it is to reach out to touch other lives.

Introduction

Ask people about their most embarrassing moment and you're likely to hear a story about how they made a fool of themselves in front of people they wanted to impress! At such times, we could swear that the universe had conspired to make us look foolish. So what gives?

The truth is that when cool and sophisticated is the goal, we can often end up being comical and nerdy instead. Part of this is trying too hard and nerves getting the best of us. For some, perhaps there's a little self-fulfilling prophecy coming into play. And, being unprepared doesn't help anyone. But the biggest reason we feel so foolish is that we take it all oh so seriously. There's a tendency to overdramatize the importance of interactions in unfamiliar social and business affairs in which we feel we come up short. Mistakes feel HUGE! So huge that you have a hard time forgetting, even years later, that you referred to the groom by his new wife's ex-boyfriend's name during your congratulatory speech, or the time you asked the adorable guy you had just met what he did for a living and when he said garbage collector you laughed and told him to stop kidding you . . . when he wasn't.

In the short term, keeping perspective can help manage your frustration level and limit the duration of self-berating. For long-term success, having some small talk social skills in your repertoire and some mingling mojo at your disposal will come in mighty handy. It makes all the difference in both the actual handling of a given situation and the way you feel about your performance. Think of it this way: Putting yourself in unfamiliar situations can be like skiing down a steep slope. If you have confidence in your skiing skills you're more likely to enjoy the challenge, to try those skills out to see what works. On the other hand, if you're up on that slippery slope with no real skills to help you down, you're apt to be intimidated. The odds also increase that you will be a little or a lot out of control on your way down. Yet even that doesn't have to be a total disaster if you have the right attitude. Being able to laugh at yourself can be a real face-saver and what you learn from missteps is always a positive outcome.

The Small Talk Handbook starts with the premise that everyone longs to be at ease, at their best, in social situations. People naturally want to be viewed as confident and astute in business encounters. This includes everyone from movie stars and CEOs to social neophytes and new employees. Even though there are those people who seem born socially savvy, most everyone gets nervous from time to time about being in unfamiliar social territory and about making the "right" impression. Preparedness goes a long way toward evening up the playing field. As does taking the attitude that social and business encounters are opportunities, a game you can have fun with once you know the rules of engagement.

The Small Talk Handbook reviews the basics of being prepared for new encounters whether they are of a romantic, friendly, or professional nature. This includes setting the tone with a helpful attitude, being aware of the body language connection, knowing how to naturally engage others with conversational prompts, and how to politely move the mingling along. *The Small Talk Handbook* lists tips for listening, being open and friendly, and knowing how much to reveal about yourself—and when. It also explores ideal interaction at work functions and how to get the most out of business relationships. This book was created to benefit women and men, of all ages, who are single or partnered, for use in both work and playful environments. Special care has been given to address issues specific to the following groups or individuals.

- Dating prospectors of any age, who are new to, awkward in, or freshly back in the dating scene
- Naturally shy people who have trouble feeling at ease in a cross section of social situations
- Interaction fumblers searching for small talk "dos" and "don'ts" tips
- Career strivers wanting to have greater impact in the business arena
- Tongue-tied romantics who lose their speaking facility in the vicinity of their heart's target
- Lackluster party mixers not getting the results they'd like from their current social interaction
- Networking novices wanting to gain tools for successfully obtaining and using business contacts
- Meek minglers ready for a more proactive participation in social encounters in order to gain greater satisfaction from social and business activities
- Business generators honing their communication skills and wanting to expand their opportunities

- Upper-echelon reactors who get nervous around "more important" peers or associates
- Image-enhancement seekers interested in being more intriguing, interesting, and appealing
- Communication enthusiasts always on the lookout for ways to improve upon and expand their interactions with other people
- New arrivals (to a new town or in a new job) needing tips for creating social connections

The Small Talk Handbook is more common sense and practical information than rocket science, which is a good thing when you only have a few minutes or so to make a dynamic first impression. It is written to be a fun read that easily enables you to access the topics most important to you. In addition, it is designed as a valuable reference you can use as you perfect your knack for chatting people up, and talking about yourself in an appealing fashion that both puts yourself and others at ease and gets you taken more seriously. Time to socialize.

CHAPTER 1

Small Talk Starter Kit

Social ease is equal parts exposure, expenditure, and experience. You can't master small talk if you don't put yourself out there. It's necessary to expose yourself to a variety of situations that call upon you to turn strangers into acquaintances, to refresh past acquaintances, and to build upon established relationships. Communication competence results from expending the necessary energy to be aware of your surroundings and the people in your personal landscape. It is affected by appropriate consideration of the place and personality, and by the effort you put into your interactions—how much you send out and how you react. Comfortable chitchatting and mingling come with experience and lots of practice. You should find yourself at greater social ease, and enjoying yourself more spontaneously and less self-consciously, as your small talk skills improve and positive experiences accrue.

Successful endeavors are usually the result of a learning process. If you aren't consciously learning you're probably repeating mistakes. Regardless of whether you are new to developing social skills, are looking for additional pointers, or need to brush up because you're newly back in the social or work world, *The Small Talk Handbook* can give you insights and new ways of thinking about your social connections. Let's start small.

SMALL TALK IS BIGGER THAN YOU THINK

Small talk often gets a bad rap. It's been trivialized and down-played as surface-speak, a time waster—but usually by people who aren't any good at it. Ask anyone who has tried and failed at small talk: Would you prefer being a fluid conversationalist or a forget-about-it geek? Most of us long to be social butterflies. We have visions of sophisticated and cool repartee. Then, sadly, the right words evade our linguistic grasp like a slippery mirage.

Forget any rocky experiences up until this moment; throw out those bitter labels you've attached to your troubled tongue. Small talk confidence is not as far out of your reach as you might think. You just need to adjust your attitude about how to approach small talk. Small is the operative word here. Little words strung together to open up communication lines between humans. Really, it's no big deal. With a little finesse, small talk can be the tool that expands your circle of friends, increases the satisfaction you feel about your social life, and puts you at ease in various business situations. It can even lead to big deals—like marriage and new clients.

But don't let it scare you; you're already engaging in small talk on a daily basis. At a time when everyone is busier than ever, more and more of our conversations have taken on a small talk personality. It is the basis of modern verbal exchange. In our rush from one activity to another, we have only a few minutes to catch up, connect with another person, and relay information. Done poorly we could end up feeling alienated from our peers, friends, neighbors, acquaintances, and coworkers. There's no emotional spark or confidence in the interaction (done in a real rush there's barely a memory of the interaction), and no real meeting of minds. Yet done correctly, with enthusiasm and true interest, these brief encounters can be the foundation for positive, helpful, and lasting relationships.

Daily modern life does, and can still further, benefit from small talk that creates a helpful network of connections. For instance, we tell friends that we long for a date and they try to set us up on blind dates, drag us off to bars and clubs, or recommend Internet sites for personals and dating. Relay your latest work project topic/crisis and friends or associates listen with interest and provide suggestions that they think may be helpful. They may offer stories about what they've done in similar situations. Or a mother mentions to her child's teacher that her reliable babysitter has moved away and the teacher recommends a neighbor's daughter. We're new in town and we ask a neighbor to recommend a good restaurant and a good dry cleaner, and soon.

What do these encounters have in common? The successful ones start with a pleasant "hello" and a smile and very little pressure to perform. Seems simple enough, so why is it that when it matters most, at a swanky party or at an important networking event, we clam up or lose our mental capacity for free-flowing thought? The most nervous among us may even sense danger in the unfamiliar rather than possibility. This causes self-protective behavior that closes us down rather than opening us up. We silently put up walls that limit our availability, even when we think we want to do just the opposite. Tension is not an energy that's inviting to other people. There are some simple rules for engagement that can be your best friends in any social situation.

YOUR SMALL TALK SURVIVAL ACCESSORIES

First, start by acknowledging that in any interaction there are factors that you cannot control: another person's personality, what they have on their mind, their schedule, the number of people in the room competing for a particular person's attention, the presence of polite and not-so-friendly cliques, and so forth. The key is to take a few SOS accessories along when you set out to make social and business connections. In this case, SOS stands for: Self-confidence, Observation prowess, and Sense of play. The potential for unplanned consequences is greatly reduced if you know that there is someone caring and loving supporting all your efforts—YOU!

SENSE OF SELF-CONFIDENCE

It goes against all our basic instincts to enter situations in which we don't know the terrain, only minimally prepared. And yet, it's impossible to avoid being in social and business events in which we don't know many, or any, people, have minimal information about who is hosting the event, how people might know each other, and how we might best fit in, and so on. The positive way to look at such an unknowable situation is as an adventure. Rather than being intimidated by such circumstances, try seeing the unlimited possibilities in such an undefined circumstance.

Starter Tips for Developing Your Small Talk Muscles

The more often you work your small talk muscles, the more responsive they become.

1. Practice on the butcher, the baker, and the candlestick maker. Start by asking advice on their area of expertise. (More about neighborly exchanges in Chapter 5.)

2. Try the topics game. Jot down topics of interest to you and try introducing them into conversation. Start with a "did you know" question or begin by saying "I ran across an article that said . . . what do you think about that?"

3. Choose a get-to-know target. If you know of someone you find intriguing or that you think would be nice to know better, make an intention to actually do it.

4. Don't hide behind being busy. If you find yourself more connected to electronics than humans, set a monthly goal for social activities.

The first rule of self-confidence is to be yourself, your real self. If you don't, it's like arriving only half dressed—frightening indeed. Just as you should pay careful attention to your attire for a date or big social event, you should prep your psyche to match your outfit. Self-confidence is your most effective accessory by far. Yes—interesting jewelry or a great tie may help (more on that later), but it's nothing compared to the aura of a confident person.

Take stock of your strengths—what you bring to the party, so to speak. People who are unduly uncomfortable in new situations may focus too heavily on their perceived faults. Try this technique: Interview yourself first before you get out and have strangers ask you questions. You may want to actually write out your responses to firmly plant in your mind all the things that you have going for you. Be clear about your answers to the following questions.

What are you good at? Assess your personality traits, natural talents, and learned skills: This may include particular subjects you've mastered like foreign languages, a personal quality such as being a good friend, or possessing a talent like playing the guitar.

What are you passionate about? Consider things that you have a current passion for as well as things you'd like to try in the future. Rock climbing or belly dancing, self-improvement or environmental cleanup, Web design or interior design. Take stock and review why they are important to you and what they add to your life.

What are your top two priorities at this moment? Be honest with yourself. This will help you shine in situations that support your priorities. For example, if you answer that building a positive reputation at work is your top priority, then understand that your actions will inevitably support that clear intention. Be confident of this rather than imagining that there are all kinds of pitfalls out there awaiting you. Likewise, if finding a mate is your top priority, appreciate your courage for putting yourself out there. Believe that the accumulation of small positive actions toward that goal is having a larger positive impact. Taking the attitude that each step is helpful, no matter what the individual outcome of any date, party, or work event, should enable you to relax a bit in these normally stress-inducing circumstances.

What do you like to do for fun? It's a question that will come up, especially in social situations, so know what puts the *joie de vivre* in your life. Perhaps you go to car races or like to play tennis. You may go to museums or hunt for collectibles on eBay. Any hobbies? (I know a guy who builds robots, and another who writes and records his own songs.) If you don't have a lot of fun to report, then realize this is an area in your life that needs immediate attention. You could respond: "Going to parties and meeting interesting people," while you work on getting a real, well-rounded life.

What are your favorite things? Think of categories like music/musicians, movies/actors, television programs, sports, types of environments (the beach versus the mountains), places to travel, colors, plants/flowers, kinds of foods, architecture styles, to name a few—anything that positively impacts your existence. Just thinking about all the things that you admire and love should put you in a happy frame of mind for a social or business event.

What is the one thing you'd like to change? This could be a physical aspect such as your height or limberness. Know why you want to change this aspect: You're attracted to tall women or you just wish you could get into all the yoga positions. You may want to change an exterior feature of your life, such as what you do for a living or where you live. Know what's stopping you from making such a change.

Once you finish your self-review, keep these personal aspects and responses in mind. This exercise should reinforce your confidence level by bringing to light your many positive qualities as well as provide plenty of fascinating fodder for conversation. It may also pinpoint personal areas that you can work on improving for even more self-confidence.

SEEING THE POSITIVE IN YOUR LEAST FAVORITE TRAITS

To better accept all your qualities, practice seeing the more positive points of any given quality—which may be valuable assets to skillful interactions. You're more likely to live the beneficial aspects if you make a point of identifying what those are and considering how you might embrace those aspects more fully. Personality traits are not static. You can gently alter how they are expressed. Change is your assurance of this. Here are a few traits that people may feel hold them back socially, and examples of the various potential manifestations of that trait, ranging from negative to positive.

Shyness

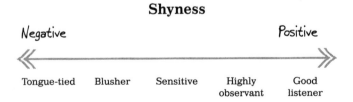

Negative				Positive
Tongue-tied	Blusher	Sensitive	Highly observant	Good listener

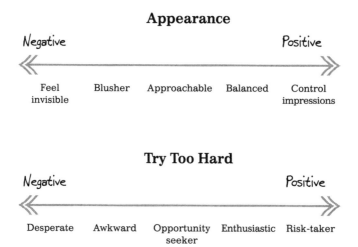

Appearance

Negative   Positive

| Feel invisible | Blusher | Approachable | Balanced | Control impressions |

Try Too Hard

Negative   Positive

| Desperate | Awkward | Opportunity seeker | Enthusiastic | Risk-taker |

OBSERVATION PROWESS

Sometimes we get so self-focused in new situations that we lose our powers of simple observation. That frantic mental checklist is to blame: "How do I look?" "Who do I know?" "Should I get a drink first?" Yet, observation is one of your most useful skills at any social or business event. It will work wonders from start to finish. A little initial surveillance enables you to assess the room, to calmly decide on your initial step, and to enter the "action" feeling grounded. During interaction, awareness lets you assess how you're doing, to make adjustments, to try different tactics. Some silent scrutiny will also help to let you know when it's a good time to move on as you mingle, and will help hone your instincts about when it's time to depart.

Taking deep breaths every now and again will keep you calm and give you the two- to- three-second lull that you need to assess your interaction. Also, aware breathing helps you to be present in the moment and more in control of the pace of the interaction. Sometimes we can feel like we have madly dashed through a moment or even through an entire evening—it's that "what just happened?" or "What did I say?" scenario.

A little light surveillance work can also provide you with information for starting conversations:

- "Who's that woman over there in the red dress?"
- "What a great turnout, did you think this party would be so happening?"
- "Great decorations/fun theme. Do you know who is responsible/how they came up with it?"
- "I once went to a party where . . . "

It's a good idea before going to any event to resolve to keep the observations positive. You never know who's responsible for particular aspects of an event (the food you just criticized was catered by the man you're speaking with) or just who knows whom. Judgments and putdowns are bad conversation crutches, and not many people are thrilled to engage in negativity for long. You want to generate an upbeat aura, not chalk up bad social karma. And if you meet a person who revels gleefully in seeing how many people they can "cut down to size," then this is not someone who will be a positive addition to your circle of acquaintances. This may go against what you see in sitcoms in which characters throw around witty but slightly or outright cruel remarks and happily dish the dirt. In real life, we don't have scriptwriters directing the action, nor laugh tracks, so it's better not to employ negative comments as an entrée to conversation.

It doesn't work well at work or play as a long-term strategy so why get associated with an attitude that has no shelf life.

SENSE OF PLAY

For those who get nervous in social situations, being light-hearted can seem like a tough task to pull off. But outlook is everything. Your perception and outlook going into any interaction will greatly determine the outcome. Working it too hard or taking it too seriously can be a death knell for fluid, fun interchange. Your attitude is transmitted whether you intend it or not. People will subconsciously pick up on it. Trying to be joyful about who you are and where you are, even if you're a bit nervous, helps ensure you send out good energy.

See where a positive, even downright cheerful, outlook leads. In many ways we are like children each time we learn something new and each time we initiate a new process that is unfamiliar to us from our past experience. The truth is, we don't really know what's going to happen. There is vast potential for what can be experienced in a new context, and with new people. So, embrace the newness with a child's enthusiasm and curiosity. In social situations, people are generally there to have an enjoyable time so assume you are part of a happy equation.

Most important, manage your expectations ahead of time. Don't go into a small talk situation—a party, a blind date, or a business association luncheon—feeling that if x, y, and z doesn't happen it was a waste of time. Try considering any outcome as acceptable, and certainly as much better than not having endeavored in the first place. Socializing is a lifelong learning experience. When you have specific expectations and they aren't met exactly as you expect, you set yourself up for feeling like a failure.

Small talk confidence is all about baby steps. Take a step, steady yourself, look around, and contemplate the next step. Concentrate on only one step and you have less to fear. Likewise, business networking is about incremental relationship-building phases. You start with a foundation; you make appraisals and adjustments as you progress, constantly fine-tuning your skills, as appropriate, for different relationships. It's not realistic to try to build an entire networking structure at a single event.

Begin by being committed to seeing all situations as opportunities: for play, for meeting interesting people, for expanding your social universe (think six degrees of separation), for injecting color into your days, for growing the spectrum of what is possible in your life. The good news is that if you have trouble feeling light and carefree at first you can fake it until the genuine emotions begin to permeate your performance. This doesn't mean you aren't being yourself; you're merely employing a tactic to curtail those dominating nerves from overpowering all your other great qualities.

Think of self-confidence, observation prowess, and a sense of play as personal coaches that help ensure a successful result. Your small talk SOS kit should help to advance those first introductions, first dates, first days at work, and first business meetings to a natural next level.

CHAPTER 2

Talking It Up with Body Language

One of the reasons that small talk is so effective is that a few words actually go a long way in conversation. How far? Would it surprise you to know that body language and communication experts widely reference a formula (established by UCLA psychology professor Albert Mehrabian in the late 1960s) that states communication is 55 percent body language, 38 percent tone of voice, and only 7 percent actual words. So, actions do indeed speak more loudly than words.

From the moment we lock eyes with someone or more formally meet them, our body language is sending out messages. Our bodies reinforce and support what we say, communicating even when we're not actually speaking aloud.

Body language can inform us about both the diverse ways we express ourselves and about the commonalities we share in communicating. Temperament shows up in physical signaling.

Certain universal body language signals spring out of inborn responsive instincts, according to body language expert Glenn Livingston, PhD, author of the ebook *How to Use Body Language*, and CEO of Psy Tech Inc. Most people grimace when in pain, smile when happy, and frown in sorrow. Yet many bodily expressions are injected into our repertoire (usually unconsciously by us) by cultural conditioning, individual experience, exposure to other people (especially our families and people of influence), and our distinct personality. Since it has a large learned behavior component, everyone can use body language to purposefully enhance communication effectiveness.

First, become aware of your body language. Do you like how you physically move and react in conversation? Are you at ease when you enter a room? How about when you're interacting with a range of personalities? If you want to improve upon your unconscious gestures and movements for better communication, start small. Trying too many things at once can look strangely obvious to people who know you, as well as interfere with your ability to listen. Like an actor who begins blocking out his or her physical movements on a stage to support the dialogue, it takes practice for the words and conscious body movements to flow together to the point of becoming more organic, comprising of both conscious movements and natural reactions. Here are a few basic pointers that any astute conversationalist should be aware of.

FROM THE NECK UP

Begin focusing on body language at face level, where expressions inform. The face is, after all, a highly sensitive barometer that reveals emotion and thoughts in fairly obvious ways. Only someone keen on projecting a poker face will consciously hide intention and emotion (and not be very interesting to interact with unless you're actually playing cards). For the rest of us, the face is full of between-the-lines content, unspoken agendas, immediate responses, and an orchestra of emotions.

Sure there are times you wish you could hide the emotions washing over you. Why does toilet paper always seem to stick to the shoe of the person who will find it most embarrassing? Our faces may indeed betray us on those occasions when it's not to our advantage to have our feelings plainly revealed. Hiding distaste or dislike can be a challenge. And yet in the course of human relations it is more often advantageous to have an animated face rather than an inscrutable one—a feat most people can't pull off regardless. Know what to look for and what to express facially as you begin decoding the language of the body and then practice incorporating helpful aspects.

SEE EYE-TO-EYE

Eyes are said to be the windows of the soul. At the very least, they can tell you whether someone is speaking from the heart. Also, the eyes are wonderfully expressive indicators of comfort level and degree of interest.

What to do: Direct eye contact is important in order to establish a connection with someone, to show respect, and to make others feel comfortable. Eye contact indicates that you are interested in another person or what they have to say. Generally, maintaining eye contact for about two-thirds of the time you spend in conversation is ideal. Less than that and you run the risk of communicating that you are uninterested, uncomfortable (having a hard time expressing feelings or feel that your personal space is being invaded), distracted, or even lying. A good listener typically maintains more eye contact than the speaker, and people rarely hold eye contact for longer than two or three seconds before glancing away. Of course, most everyone gets distracted now and again—by something happening in close proximity to us, when we catch something out of the corner of our eye or by a loud noise. You want to put people at ease with eye contact, not give the impression that you have blinders on.

Because our eyes are such wonderful communication tools we knowingly and automatically use them to reinforce the intent behind our words. Eyes are expert conveyers (in concert with brows) of emotions like concern, gratitude, puzzlement, fear, fascination, questioning, pleading, and joy. Consciously or unconsciously we look to the eyes to ascertain whether what we hear is true. So it's wise to be sure that our own communiqués are reinforced with the eyes.

Sometimes nerves can make a smile feel forced, especially in new social situations. Let your smile reach your eyes and the friendly warmth you're extending will be received as authentic. Laughing eyes and twinkling eyes are highly appealing because they indicate an abundance of happiness or mirth. When someone is excited they widen their eyes and the pupils dilate.

Therefore, they are highly effective for gaining attention for both your verbal and nonverbal messages. The charming flirt knows how to use his or her eyes to advantage.

What not to do: If you're in conversation, it's very impolite to scan a crowd or watch people coming in the door over someone's shoulder. A twitching or darting eye may be seen as a lying eye (don't let dry contacts send the wrong message). People blink frequently when they are anxious, scared, bored, or tired, according to John Stern, PhD, a pioneer in research on blinking and professor emeritus of psychology at Washington University in St. Louis. These are not especially positive aspects to communicate. And, if someone narrows her eyes à la Clint Eastwood, she is feeling threatened.

READ MY LIPS

Lips are highly user-friendly for putting others at ease. Sometimes all it takes is a simple smile. And yet, it seems that many of us have gotten into the habit of parceling out our smiles. We save them for "safe" recipients we're fairly sure will smile back. We save smiles for when we have the time. It may seem silly to those who always have a smile on their faces, but some of us need more practice to naturally respond with a smile to a range of situations. Instances in which a smile would be helpful:

- When you desire to show encouragement
- When you want to be silently supportive
- To reflect obvious gladness to be in someone's company
- To speed along the process of someone warming up to you
- When you'd like to be seen as charming
- To indicate a fun-to-get-to-know nature

What to do: Get into the habit of smiling at people whether you are exchanging words or not. Smile as you pass strangers on the street, smile when you meet with colleagues, smile when you enter a room at a social function. It will become a more integral part of your demeanor. If you do this enough, your smile may even become a key part of how people think of you. A smile automatically communicates interest in other people. In return you're likely to be perceived as approachable, friendly, and confident.

A few essentials about other "lip shtick" you should consider. Wet your lips and part them slightly and really there's little need to say more. This conveys sexual interest as loudly as the call of the mating moose. That's strong language so be sure you're using it on the intended person. Pursed lips convey disapproval. Anger is evident in compressed lips. Thoughtful lips twist to one side, while someone biting his or her lips shows nervousness or anxiety.

What not to do: Don't make the mistake of believing that a super-cool person doesn't smile or show emotion. You'll end up coolly alone or will attract all the wrong types (i.e., people who see disinterest as a challenge or people who can't tell cool from codependent). Miscommunication is the name of that game. Brave showing a bit of your true self; it's your best long-term strategy.

HEADS UP

The head and neck combo is very adaptable to nonverbal communication. We nod approval and agreement, and to indicate that we're paying attention. We shake our head "no," to indicate disagreement or disbelief. When we keep a level head we are in control, self-assured, authoritative even. A tilted head is more relaxed and friendly. Head tilts to one side express thoughtful consideration and show active listening. A tilt one way and then another may correlate to asking a question. We tilt our head bringing our chins down for emphasis of statements like, "I just don't get it." We throw our heads back in laughter. And, a flip of the head/hair is a standard flirting motion.

What to do: Use nonverbal cues when you're the listener. Leave a favorable impression by receiving the other person's remarks with visible interest. Show that you are in sync with what they are saying. A nod of the head every now and again accomplishes this simply and quite effectively. You can subtly mimic the speaker's head movements—a tilt to one side or the other, or by raising your chin. This is called mirroring (more on that later) and further reinforces that you are on the same page.

What not to do: Don't hold yourself stiffly without making head movements; relax your neck and shoulders. When you don't send body language signals for others to receive, consciously or unconsciously, you make them uncomfortable, nervous even. You don't want to come off as zombie-like.

NOW HEAR THIS!

As previously mentioned, for effective communication words are dependent on people putting their whole bodies into it. This includes using the vocal cords. How we say something breathes life into word meaning. Our voice goes up at the end of a sentence when we pose a question; lowered to a whisper and the statement is a secret; high-pitched and shrill and a comment becomes an accusation.

It's well documented that vocal cues have a major role in compelling and accurate communication. All you need do is watch a child/parent interaction involving discipline and you can pretty plainly see the huge role tone of voice plays in the message that the child receives. Good debaters excel in controlling the tone and tempo of a conversation. Effective communicators pluck from the wonderful range of vocal "keys" at their disposal.

What to do: If showing a range of emotions with your voice is not second nature, you'll need to practice matching your tone to the intent behind your words. Try reading out loud to hear how you sound to yourself. Experiment with modulating your tone to include high, midrange, and lower intonations. This will help to ensure that you keep listeners engaged and that they "get" the true feelings behind your words. For example, when we speak intimately with a loved one, we tend to speak more softly or with a deeper timbre. Words spoken for the purpose of clarification may be spoken firmly, slowly, and with added emphasis put on important words. The opinions we voice are usually packed with strong emotions clearly communicated by our tone of voice.

Use voice tone to accentuate what you say, but without startling the other person. Show excitement if you're making a strong point or relaying a great story/joke:

- "That's hilarious! It reminds me of the time . . . "
- "I can't believe you said that! I've always thought that too."

A lowered tone, in sync with leaning in toward a person, reinforces your interest and enhances the possibility for emotional closeness. Alternately, we inherently want to keep our distance from people we don't like or when we want to clearly communicate a lack of interest or disinclination to share "space" with another.

Again, words are only 7 percent of what is conveyed during a conversation; 38 percent is tone and intonation. Relax into letting your voice flex its natural vocal range. This is especially important if you have feelings of not being effectively heard. By being vocally more assertive and using ear-catching intonation, a few words will go a long way.

What not to do: Don't talk too loudly or too close to someone. Nothing is more off-putting than someone you are in close proximity to talking at a sustained fever pitch. And don't talk too quietly either. People shouldn't have to struggle to hear you.

HAND IN HAND

The hands are amazing instruments of communication. You don't have to be a palmist to glimpse a person's personality from the way they use their hands. From the wave of a hand to the handshake, from fidgeting to a light caress, there's clear meaning in those hand gestures (I'm sure most of you can think of a few not generally displayed in polite company). Everyday words in the English language point up the positive use of the hands: hands-on, handily, and handy.

What to do: The handshake is often your first physical contact with another person. Whether you're in a social or business context use a firm, not wishy-washy grip. This conveys a healthy confidence and sincere pleasure in meeting someone. Be wary of the person who turns your vertically extended hand over flat so that the top of your hand faces the ground and their hand is on top. This person is aggressively declaring: "I'm dominant here; I'm in charge." It's an inauspicious way to begin a conversation or a genuine two-sided relationship. This person is not overly concerned with equality.

To convey openness and friendliness, talk with your palms facing somewhat upwards. Some people touch their palms together to emphasize a point. Tossing your palms up may accentuate feelings of humility or uncertainty, such as an "I just don't know?" sentiment. A hand or both hands extended toward a listener or listeners can reinforce a call for support.

In work situations, with superiors or people you don't know well, be aware of the other person's gestures. This makes it possible for you to show with your own mirroring gestures that you understand their attitude or the corporate climate. For instance, if superiors use their hands as they talk, in all likelihood they will be receptive to you doing the same.

Expressing yourself with palms facing downward is generally viewed as a more assertive or aggressive movement. Often people will lay their palms flat on a table for emphasis or repeatedly raise a hand up and down to make a strong point. Some people use a chopping motion with their hand to reinforce the idea that "this is the way I believe business works best," or a "this is the way things are" kind of sentiment.

Touching in a nonthreatening way—a light touch of the hand, a brush against an arm—can effectively show romantic interest and encourage a like response. Appropriate context is important for touching. When you initiate physical contact, observe the reaction: surprise, acceptance, reciprocation, or withdrawal. Does the person maintain the distance or move back? A particularly painful episode of *The Bachelor* featured a woman being very touchy during a date to the obvious discomfort of the guy. He actually seemed to recoil, and yet, determinedly she kept at her strategy even though it was failing miserably (she did not make the cut). Interaction is a two-sided dance. Make sure you're not all about "advancing" your goal rather than engaging in leading and following, acting and responding.

What not to do: Don't use your hands so much that you distract people completely from what you're saying.

Wringing your hands, clutching your forearms, or obviously not knowing what in the world to do with suddenly awkward appendages called hands will make you look nervous and tense. Some nervous gesturing can be read as lying, too.

ALL ARMS AND LEGS

Arms quite clearly convey whether you are approachable or off-limits. Arms comfortably by your sides or behind your back say that you are inviting connection. Arms in a relaxed manner indicate ease with interaction: In a standing position hands might be calmly clasped and arms relatively straight; seated you might rest your elbows and forearms on the arms of a chair. With family and loved ones we open our arms wide in invitation to say, "Give me a hug." Alternately, your arms can act as your nonverbal safety shield. If they're crossed, especially across your chest, you are communicating a restricted availability or showing defensiveness.

What to do: Be aware of your natural conversational style. In conversation outgoing people are more likely to use big gestures, while quieter personality types tend to limit their gestures.

Evaluate yourself. Are you being too in control or using too little space? Could you be a more effective speaker by increasing arm motions to emphasize your enthusiasm, to connect to someone, or to make a point? Alternately, perhaps you use your hands to the extreme and need to tone it down. Are you known to accidentally hit passing waiters and whap guests standing in close proximity?

Not only are arms great for hugging, they can be invaluable assets in getting a romantic spark going. In flirting, a woman might expose her wrist in the wave of a hand as she speaks or as she holds a drink. This speaks to being open, vulnerable, and available.

What not to do: Put elbows on a tabletop and tap fingers, fidget, crook your arm to look at your nails, or tightly intertwine fingers. Such movements convey unappealing things like: "I'm impatient," "I'm restless," "I'm bored," or "I'm tense." When you are speaking and you see these physical signals being made by the listener, pause so that they can speak or ask for their input.

Legs have the square inch advantage. Because there is generally so much real estate involved, leg positions get noticed. Who can forget the *Basic Instinct* scene in which Sharon Stone crosses and uncrosses her legs as a power play that rivets all eyes on her? Does anyone remember what she was saying?

What to do: Crossing and uncrossing the legs slowly is in almost every flirt's repertoire. Stroke the thighs at the same time and you are inviting touch, basically saying: "Wouldn't you like to touch me like this?" To show interest, face your knees toward the person of attraction.

Poetic Praise for Body Language

Throughout the ages, literature and songs have celebrated the power of individual body parts to speak volumes:

> "An eye full of gentle salutations—and soft
> responses . . . "
>
> —Laurence Sterne

> "Did not the heavenly rhetoric of thine eye,
> 'Gainst whom the world cannot
> hold argument,
> Persuade my heart to this false perjury?"
>
> —*Love's Labour's Lost*, William Shakespeare

> "She is Venus when she smiles;
> But Juno when she walks,
> And Minerva when she talks."
>
> —Ben Jonson

On the other hand, quickly crossing and uncrossing the legs shows impatience or nervousness and can be distracting. Tapping the toes ditto. In business it's recommended that you keep legs uncrossed or crossed at the ankles for women and lean forward a bit. Crossing the leg with a foot resting on the knee and leaning back should be reserved for more casual situations.

What not to do: Don't stand on one leg—either with the other foot on top of the standing foot or entwined around the standing leg. This displays insecurity, discomfort in standing on one's own two feet. It's difficult to feel grounded in this stance, which puts you at a disadvantage in a social or business situation in which you want to be ready to take action or react to what is happening in a fully present manner. Also, be aware of rocking or standing in an impatient manner, such as standing with one or both hands on a pushed out hip, and having one leg placed further forward with a tapping toe pointing outward.

POSTURE AND POSES

Whether or not your mother got around to correcting your posture, believe in its power: Standing up straight is immensely important to a positive image. Good posture with shoulders back and head held high presents most everyone in the best light. It is a welcoming stance, and indicates confidence. Someone who stands tall and pushes out his chest is looking to increase his sphere of influence, to literally make a "bigger" impression. You don't have to imitate Dudley Do Right, but don't be too small in the space that you occupy either. You want to project a positive presence.

What to do: Keeping your chin and head up helps you stay positive and to be received that way. Looking down, one can get lost in negative thoughts and literally lose visual contact with the other people in a room. At a party or business event, let your walk and your body help you project the attitude that you're an asset to the gathering.

The way you hold yourself is important in displaying confidence and comfort in your own body. It's pretty natural to turn toward someone who interests us and away from those we don't want to give our attention to. This shows that we've chosen a person as a focus and we are open to further exchange. Turning toward someone also puts you in a good position to initiate additional closeness such as leaning in toward them, as well as knee and leg touching if you are sitting or arm touching if you are standing.

What not to do: Slouching communicates weakness, lack of stature, and insecurity. Bad postures show a lack of "spine." Leave the hunched shoulders at home. A rigid body posture is plainly uninviting as it communicates feelings of inferiority or anxiousness.

Some poses are body language one-liners—nothing subtle going on at all. For instance, hands on the hips and legs firmly planted brags of super confidence, a take-charge attitude. Crossed arms and a sidelong glance with a raised eyebrow plainly expresses that "I'm not buying this." Men use poses that flex their muscles when they want to show off and clearly indicate sexual attraction, just as a woman may sit or stand in a way that emphasizes what she considers her most appealing body part.

Words That Speak Volumes

Most body-related references easily produce mental visuals—positive and negative—that make the phrases easily understood:

- Arms wide open
- Chin up
- Eyeball-to-eyeball
- Handholding
- Keep your distance
- My lips are sealed
- Poker faced
- Pull your leg
- Stone faced
- Standing tall

MIRRORING OR SYNCHRONIZING WITH OTHERS

Mirroring is basically following someone's lead in terms of tone of voice, hand motions, leg or arm positions (crossed or uncrossed), head tilts, and so forth. Used effectively, mirroring is meant to send a message of flattery, a supportive way of showing that you are in sync with another person. In business, mirroring can send a subtle message that you recognize the dynamics of the group. In an interview it may help you be perceived as a good fit for an organization. A word of caution: Don't try to mimic every move a person makes. The most important thing to remember about body language is that it must be taken in context. It should be weighed against other factors such as the specific situation, the personality of the person, the actual words, and what your instincts are telling you. These elements should support the body language signals you pick up. Take into consideration your relationship to the person. You may need to consider what other dynamics are going on during the interaction as well as any cultural and gender differences that affect body language perception. Use intentional body language cues in various contexts and see what a difference it makes to the quality of your interactions. Enhanced body language awareness should help to put you at greater ease in social situations, and help you create tighter connections with people. With practice and time, you'll find yourself more persuasive and confident.

What body language won't do is put a good face on a bad attitude. In his email newsletter, Dr. Livingston states that, "people have built-in B.S. detectors." Not many people will be taken in by a big smile if the true feelings behind the smile are negative. If you try to use body language cues to misrepresent your genuine feelings or to stand in for authentic beliefs, you will probably come off as false.

That's the great thing about body language: It can be extremely helpful in communicating true feelings, but it generally doesn't provide a very good false cover for fakers with less-than-honorable intentions.

CHAPTER 3

Savvy Socializing

As children we learn how to socialize first within the family dynamic and then in our neighborhoods and at school. We try out social skills as part of a group before we advance to one-on-one encounters. Ideally this progression goes smoothly and helps to instill you with self-confidence and a lively sense of adventure in your social relations.

On the other hand, if your family tended toward dysfunctional interaction or your peers embraced a rebel or outcast identity, you may have a few oh-so-minor lapses in your social education. And, of course, personality plays a significant role in interpersonal communications. But, whether you are correcting less-than-helpful life experiences or looking to improve upon your inborn social nature, awareness and practice are your best allies.

EVALUATING YOUR SOCIAL SKILLS

How do you feel about your social skills? Up to this point we've discussed small talk strategies and body language skills that you can take along with you on social activities. Just like a hostess gift you arrive with, everyone has something valuable to bring to the party in terms of attitude, physical presence, conversation style, personal revelation, and response to others. It's important to know your strengths and weaknesses in these areas so you can focus on specific ways to refine or glam up your social panache. Keep in mind whether or not you're bringing a desirable asset to the party or something better left at home. Some clarifying questions you should ask yourself include:

Attitude—Do you try to be positive or do you bring whatever you are feeling to the occasion with you? Do you believe in your ability to create social opportunities or do you see interaction as out of your hands or primarily fate-driven?

Physical presence—Generally, how do you feel about the way you look? Would an updated hairstyle or wardrobe boost help put you in a better frame of mind for socializing? How do you carry yourself? Are you aware of using your body (walking, gesturing, etc.) to reinforce your presence and messages in a social setting? Do you like to dance?

Conversation style—Do you enjoy chatting for hours or prefer more limited talk time? What do you enjoy talking about? Do you keep up to date on current events and news topics? Are you a good listener?

Personal revelation—Are you comfortable talking about yourself? Some people can reveal just about anything about themselves and their families with no apparent self-consciousness. Other people are more apt to put a happy face on all their disclosures. Do you easily talk about your skills or expertise? Are you honest with yourself and others?

Response—How do you respond to others? Do you think that you're perceived as kindhearted, empathetic, supportive, or nonjudgmental? Are you complimentary of others?

Reviewing these essential personality areas can be insightful for you. We can get into a pattern of thinking about ourselves as one "type" of person. Often we too harshly judge our perceived personality type and think of it as unalterable. We're each so fantastically multilayered. To a great extent, we choose which aspects of our total personality we try to bring out or to show at any given time. Examining your traits in a more positive light, you may find that being more of a good listener and less a lead talker can serve you well in your relationships, as long as you don't hide behind the listening role. While our essence doesn't change, life circumstances and experiences do color our personalities for good and bad. Reviewing one's strengths and weaknesses is not for the purpose of self-judgment. It's for clarity, so you can focus on the particular steps that will help garner the results you desire.

RECOGNIZING YOUR CONVERSATION STYLE

To help you identify your current conversation style, take this brief, just-for-fun quiz.

CONVERSATION STYLE QUIZ

1. What phrase sums up your attitude about social interactions?

   a. Life is a stage and I'm the star.
   b. What's not to like?
   c. I'm all ears.
   d. I like to watch.

2. Who are you conversationally?

   a. You tend to hold court, leading a conversation and keeping your audience enthralled with your life dramas or uproariously laughing at your wit and humor.
   b. You enjoy conversing and can find something to say on most subjects.
   c. You are a good listener, interjecting comments judiciously when you think you have something pertinent to add.
   d. You're more comfortable letting others do the talking.

3. What do you like to talk about?

   a. Yourself and your adventures.
   b. Trivia, movies, music, sports, "in the news" topics, and people.

   c. More meaty topics of discussion such as other peoples'
personal stories, the role humans have in affecting the
future of the planet, the importance of voting, and so on.

   d. You're not sure. You usually let other people bring up
topics.

4. How receptive and responsive are you to other speakers?

   a. What other speakers?

   b. Other peoples' comments keep the conversation
charged and flowing!

   c. You naturally make empathetic and supportive
comments and responses.

   d. You have much you could be saying in response to
others but few words actually come out.

5. What is your conversation goal usually?

   a. To be the most amusing and entertaining in the room.

   b. To help make the conversation lively and interesting.

   c. Quality over quantity. Making good connections with a
few people.

   d. To fit in and not make a fool of myself.

6. How do you feel after most of your interactions?

   a. Self-satisfied.

   b. Energized and happy.

   c. Glad of having met some really interesting people.

   d. Regretful that I didn't say more.

ANALYZING YOUR SCORE

Three or more responses for any one letter (a, b, c, or d) indicates a propensity toward a primary conversational style. You may bounce between a couple of conversational styles depending on your mood and the personalities of the other people you're socializing with (e.g., sometimes you give up the floor when someone else is "on" or to a guest of honor). Keep in mind that just because you currently exhibit one style doesn't mean you can't move toward another modus operandi. To a great extent, everyone has control over the personal qualities he or she projects and how they are perceived. You don't have to be quiet and meek. You can be quietly friendly. You don't have to be loud and brash, you can be lively and generous. Add up your responses and review these brief definitions of typical conversation styles.

A. The Performer—You highly regard an audience more than you strive for balanced interaction. You're comfortable in the limelight and can get restless if you're not leading the conversation. Often exceedingly entertaining, you certainly take conversation pressure off the group or your date. Be aware that your social dominance can run the risk of being perceived as narcissistic after a while. People may get bored if they don't feel there's a place for them in the "action." Watch for people's reactions, and practice using your extroverted personality to draw others out and hear what they have to say.

B. Easy Chatterer—You read various publications and are aware of what's happening in the news and with cultural trends, finding it fairly easy to use information in conversation. You come off as friendly and upbeat. Watch interjecting those interesting facts or comments too often or out of context, especially when others have the floor and are trying to take the conversation in a particular direction.

C. Good Listener—While you speak up in conversation, you enjoy really listening to other people, showing support and letting them know that you are interested. You're seen as empathetic and easy to be around. Sometimes you may be just a bit of a mystery. Appraise whether or not you could be revealing more about yourself, perhaps in order for others to sense a shared connection or outlook, or for others to glimpse a refreshing point of view.

D. Quietly Present—Just because you're not comfortable talking yourself up doesn't mean that you'd rather stay at home. You may try to get out and meet people, it's just not second nature to you. As hard as it is for you to fathom, people who don't understand your nature may misinterpret your quietness as arrogance or as your being judgmental. This means that you have to work a little harder to enhance your social skills so that you're more vocal. Just because you've been quiet in the past doesn't mean you can't bring out more of yourself in the future.

Use categories like these only as guidelines. Avoid labeling yourself or letting other people label you. No one is all one great personality trait or completely one character flaw. When we stay open to the presence of opportunities (and stop seeing closed doors), each of us has the potential to be more fully what we'd like to be.

SETTING THE SCENE FOR SUCCESS

Like most endeavors, socializing has a natural lifecycle: a beginning, middle, and end. If you're savvy you recognize the phases as well as take responsibility for your role in creating a smooth and successful interaction. The following are ten points of successful socializing that can help minimize your stress and maximize your personal flair.

1. DRESS APPROPRIATELY FOR THE OCCASION

Nothing makes you feel more comfortable in your own skin than knowing you're looking good and appropriately dressed for the occasion. If you need to, check with the hostess or party giver about any dress code guidelines. If you're going to a new club or unfamiliar social scene that you're not sure about, call the establishment and ask about dress guidelines. Nothing can put you off your stride easier than arriving somewhere unprepared for coat and tie requirements or finding yourself under or overdressed.

Accessories like bold or unique jewelry create a focus that people you meet can easily comment upon to start up a conversation. For men an eye-catching or themed tie (at more formal events like weddings, the opera or ballet, and after work get-togethers) can spark a first comment. A dynamic ring, perhaps one handed down in your family, is a good accent that can start a personal conversation.

2. BE A FULLY PRESENT PERSON

Patty Duff, a party entertainer in Seattle, is an expert at sizing up a room and engaging guests in interactive games. She advises: "When you enter a room take your space; be present in the space you are occupying and people will be drawn to you." Nothing is more attractive than confidence and a face that expresses, "I'm glad to be here."

3. FEEL YOUR BODY

Breathe. Feel grounded as you walk tall and smile. Remember your body language is telegraphing information to the other people from the minute you're observed. What messages do you want to send? Think comfort, confidence, and fun. Fake it if you have to at first.

4. EVALUATE THE ROOM

Where's the bar or food? Do you see anyone you know? What group dynamics are in play? Any interesting individuals you might want to meet? Be aware of who catches your eye and smiles back—that's an opening. People sitting alone at bars or people in line for drinks at events make good first connections. Offer a drink-related comment, "I once heard someone order a Raspy Rapunzel—sounds like a throat burning drink with a hair in it. What's the most unusual drink name you know?" Is the action in full swing or a little quiet? Is there entertainment? Is there a specific décor style or themed decorations? Use these observations as conversation fodder when you start to mingle.

5. SELECT YOUR FIRST POINT OF CONTACT

You may want to search out the hostess, who can make some introductions. You can get a drink to give yourself a specific direction in which to head after you arrive. Look for the groups of people who seem to be enjoying themselves. Such a group makes a good first point of contact. Make eye contact with one or two people in the group and approach. If your smile is returned you'll probably be welcome to join the group. If you are unsure you can always ask: "Mind if I join you?" Don't try to join groups that are so closely encircled in conversation there is literally no space for someone new. Look for people who are alone who might appreciate a friendly hello.

6. COMMIT TO BEING POSITIVE AND JOYFUL

Attitude translates into body language and increases the chances that you'll have a good experience. Decide how long you'll stay AT A MINIMUM. An hour is a good time frame. This enables you to really look for fun and to relax past any initial awkwardness. Conversely, setting a maximum time with the attitude of "if this is boring I'm going to leave in fifteen minutes," can result in time watching instead of paying attention to potential opportunities for lively interaction. Keep yourself flexible and don't cut yourself off too soon.

7. HAVE SOME CONVERSATION STARTERS IN MIND

Think of a funny, out of the ordinary, or humbling (not depressing) personal story—an anecdote that will be received as amusing, interesting, or endearing. Have some "did you hear . . . ?" or "did you know . . . ?" tidbits of information on a popular topic or news happening that you can interject with most social groups.

8. CHALLENGE YOURSELF TO MINGLE

Once you've engaged with a person or a group for long enough to get a sense about your compatibility or to learn something about them that you can use later to restart conversation, gently disengage yourself with a warm and simple statement. Try something straightforward like "It was great talking with you, I'm going to mingle a bit," or "It was nice meeting everyone, I'm going to catch up with a friend. I hope to see you later." If you just want a few minutes to take a deep breath or to assess the situation you can offer to refill a person's drink, but this does commit you to going back. Keeping your comment as close to the truth as possible is best. If you're dealing with a mature grownup, she will understand. You are merely interested in finding out who else is at the party, club, or event, so don't be so awkward with your departure that you end up leaving a bad impression, or make the person feel self-conscious that it was something she said. You'll have a better sense about how long you want to spend with a person or group if you know ahead of time what your socializing goal is. Is it to meet one special person, to become acquainted with new people who might become part of your social circle, or to be introduced to a specific person you heard would be at the event? Just don't hang with one person because you fear making a move out of your newly created comfort zone.

9. KNOW WHAT PITFALLS TO AVOID

Pass up falling in with a gossipy group. It can be amusing at first, but may limit your social opportunities since gossips tend to alienate other people. Enjoying a good laugh at someone else's expense can also come back to bite you—like later that evening when you're mesmerized by a guy who won't give you the time of day because he overheard you laughing about him. Give yourself time to evaluate the various dynamics going on before you commit your allegiance. Also don't use the same opening line or corny joke with everyone you meet. People are funny about liking to be treated like individuals, and when you use a line or joke repeatedly you're bound to forget who has heard it already. A friend calls this "Groundhog Day Syndrome."

10. KNOW WHEN TO GRACEFULLY DEPART

You've probably heard the phrase "stayed too long at the fair." The more often you put yourself out there in various social situations, the more fine-tuned your radar will become about when you've had enough fun or just had enough period. It's sometimes tempting to stay at an event or a social mixer beyond the point that we're having a good time. When socializing begins to feel too much like a chore, or you've already made the rounds, it's a good time to leave. And, the more introverted your nature the easier it is to feel stimuli overload. It's not a good thing to be the one who closes down a club or bar, or who is the last to leave a party as the host sleepily escorts you to the door. If you've made a point of connecting with people, there shouldn't be a need to hang out and get that certain person's phone number (you should have it already or already tried) or to make sure someone specific notices you (assume they noticed and weren't interested). Such tactics reek of desperation. Don't go there.

There are times when small talk savvy and mingling confidence can be helped along by bringing a friend to a social gathering. Friends provide an initial comfort zone. They may be able to introduce you to people they know or join you in making that first point of contact. But don't stay side-by-side all night long. You want to hone your solo social skills. And, hopefully, you'll have lots to talk about when you meet up again.

FIRST IMPRESSIONS

It's a reasonable goal to want to fall on the positive end of the social impact meter, but no one appeals to every person and that's okay. Your power is in understanding the dynamics of interactions so that you put your energy into what you can control.

First impressions are often formed about us even before we speak. So, perspective is important on this point. While a first impression is important since it oils the wheels of the subsequent interaction, despite what you've heard, it isn't everything. It isn't your whole life or even your only chance. In fact, it's been known to happen that people who at first dislike each other for one reason or another (who can remember?) can come to change their minds and become friends or even marry.

A first impression is just the first thing that transpires in one particular social situation. True, judgmental people may cling mean-spiritedly to their negative impression, but that's mostly about their need to feel superior. The people with whom you probably want to connect anyway are likely to be more generous about forming a conclusion. So strive for a good first impression through positive body language, an engaging demeanor, and a friendly opening line, but don't panic or bail out if you have to start again.

First impressions get filtered through actual interaction. Impressions segue into more firm perceptions based on the next few minutes of small talk. And, you can use the five key factors already mentioned—attitude, physical presence, conversation style, personal revelation, and response—to connect with others and make the "walk away" perception a positive one.

Put yourself in new social situations knowing that you will get more comfortable in them over time. I'm a firm believer that a little courage and pushing oneself beyond one's comfort point gets rewarded, sometimes immediately. In many instances you will have a "that wasn't so bad" experience, and in the long run you acquire helpful life skills and memory-bank positive results that make the next scary thing less intimidating. Hey, the good thing about going to bars, clubs, parties, and social events is that you have plenty of chances to practice. You may even want to set your goal as just doing that—practicing. It takes the pressure off when you aim high but don't set a stressful expectation or get it into your head that success is defined by one particular result.

Remember, in many cases you're dealing with strangers who don't know what you're like. It's the perfect chance to try some "stretching" exercises. Pretend a bit if it helps to bolster your nerve. For one encounter, emulate aspects of someone whose social finesse or positive attitude you admire. Start small. Try out Julia Robert's big smile or Johnny Depp's playful manner. Does pretending a bit help to bring out more social aspects of your personality? Notice how you feel. Sometimes all it takes is trying out a certain attitude or image to actually begin living it.

Over the centuries, some of the most captivating people have been perfectly average-appearing people who have a knack for attracting people to them. What is the secret of their magnetism? They know what their strong points are and they make people comfortable. They have a sparkle in their eyes and interject a contagious aura of playful curiosity and cheer into their social interactions. While you may not be able to perfect such a devil-may-care attitude you can pay attention to better projecting your own presence. We each need to take responsibility for what we bring to personal interactions. Taking the steps you need to be as comfortable as possible in a social environment will help encourage the result you desire: being noticed and appreciated for your whole-person package.

CHAPTER
4

Social Ease on the Dating Scene

The dating world seems made up of too many people who don't think they're interesting enough and an inordinate number of individuals who totally overestimate their charisma. Dating can make many of us feel at our most vulnerable so it's easy to get stuck in a pattern of dating behavior that doesn't get great results. You're too nervous, unsure about how to act or "who" to be. Perhaps you manhandle your nerves by trying to brag your way through an encounter. In the midst of a date, it can be difficult to turn bad energy around or to strategize about what tactics (short of having a personality transplant) could create a change for the better. Do any of these sentiments sound familiar?

- An alien geek takes over your mind and mouth forcing you to say all the wrong things.
- Starting a conversation feels about as natural as bathing fully clothed—ill planned and all wet.
- You fervently hope your date has something interesting to say. Why do you always meet people who are as awkward at this as you?
- Being a girly or flirty woman does not come one bit naturally. Does dating have to be this hard?
- You told your date everything about yourself in one night. Then you feel really exposed when he doesn't call back.
- Once a date starts talking about herself, you just let her carry on, without giving much back about yourself.
- You tell your date about your many accomplishments and/or about all the great things you have. But he/she doesn't seem impressed.

You probably wouldn't have picked up this book if you didn't care tremendously about your interactions with other people and the impressions they hold of you. At the very least, you'd like to be making more connections that feel less painful than shin splints. You'd like good exchanges to lead to subsequent get-togethers, effectively expanding upon the potential you see for establishing a romantic connection or a friendly relationship. It's not a lot to ask. Like most things in life, you need to find a place to start and then take it one step at a time.

THE FOUR Ps OF SUCCESSFUL DATING: PLAN, PRIMP, PROJECT, AND PROMOTE

The good thing about dating is that it plays out in a specific time and place that you have some control over. Whether you have been asked out or did the asking, be sure to supply your input about what activities you prefer and what time of the day you'd like to meet. This helps both parties start off under the best possible circumstances, and one person doesn't find themselves in an activity that makes them feel foolish. Dates are foremost learning experiences meant to be enjoyed, regardless of whether you are meant to continue the relationship. After all, this is someone who will touch your life, even if only briefly. He'll have a bit part in your history. If you're lucky a date may tap into that mysterious intersection where hopes and desires meet up with fate. So take the time to set the scene.

PLAN

Plan an activity that puts you at ease and consider some topics to discuss. A first date between one and two hours is enough time to get to know someone. If it's not working out you haven't overextended yourself so you shouldn't have to later complain that you wasted your time or how painful each moment was. Also, being comfortable in your selected situation should help you to be respectful of the other person for the duration—showing interest and being friendly.

PRIMP

Primp to show that you care about looking attractive for the other person. Knowing we show our best selves on the outside provides some confidence that we've set the stage for bringing our best assets to the interaction.

You might want to discuss appropriate clothing if it's not clearly obvious what the dress code will be. Bad breath can be a turnoff even before you get to turn-ons. And, too much cologne or perfume reeks of trying too hard and can quite literally make you tough to get close to.

Primping should extend to your living space if you're having your date over to your place. Patricia from Seattle recalled an especially "impressionable" date with a guy she had seen socially and whose good looks and humor had bowled her over. When she got in his car the ashtray was overflowing, there was trash and junk everywhere. Instead of romantic notions, she began to wonder if he used deodorant, what his shower looked like, and if he ever cleaned the sheets on his bed.

PROJECT

Project your true personality and interests in a sincere manner, while encouraging the other person to talk about himself by asking open-ended questions. How much is the person willing to reveal about what matters to him? Does the answer seem sincere, or is it what he thinks you want to hear? In this case, he answered that he'd like to go on a hike up a mountain that ended in a beautiful view, where they could picnic on champagne, shrimp, and chocolates. Her take: He liked the rugged outdoors and physical activity but also enjoyed the finer pleasures in life like good food and drink. He was down to earth and romantic!

Balance your listening with talking, and vice versa. It's always tempting to let the more outgoing person do all the talking.

Yet when you project your "light" self, a poor paltry portion, your date may end up feeling emotionally undernourished or self-conscious about having talked too much.

PROMOTE

Promote yourself positively. We are each our own best public relations person. What are your best qualities or talents? How would your best friend describe you? Keep your answers in mind as you interact, so that your nonverbal cues are positive and upbeat. Give voice to these qualities as the occasion presents itself. Better yet, create the occasion by asking your date a question related to the quality you'd like to share. Then when it's your turn to interject a comment you have the perfect opening. For instance ask, "What do you enjoy doing in your spare time?" Then when your date turns the question back to you, you can say, "I like to get together with my friend Tom and play guitar. We jam and make up songs on the spot. It's more humorous than serious song making but we get a kick out of it." You've told your date that you're musical, creative, and have an engaging sense of play—all of which can be traits that are hard to display on a date when you're less than your most comfortable self.

Balance information about things that you "do" in your life (accomplishments) with how you "feel" about particular aspects of your life or events happening in the world. Reveal something about what inspires you or what you get a kick out of and about the direction of your hopes. The four Ps provide opportunities for showing how much you give of yourself. While you don't want to overdo it, you do want your date to have an accurate idea about your emotional availability and your ability to give and receive attention and affection.

COMMUNICATION DYNAMICS

Communication dynamics respond well to straightforward action, but nerves, self-consciousness, and self-judgment often complicate the outcome. The key is to feel increased confidence that you have the tools for feeling in control on the surface. Then, while you may still sense the nerves inside, they won't be running the show.

THE SILENT MOVIE CONNECTION

Again, remember that communication is partly subconscious and instinctual; we pick up on peoples' positive or negative energy, and instantaneously interpret body language cues. So watch your own body language and be aware of your date's physical cues. Walk tall (no rounded shoulders or downcast eyes) and smile. Research shows that women are naturally more physically expressive than guys, gesturing up to twice as often. Understanding this basic gender difference helps ensure more accurate readings of body language cues. The key is context: Does it seem general or targeted?

Once engaged in small talk, maintain appropriate eye contact and face the person you're attracted to. Be aware of gestures and postures that give you clues about how you're doing and how the person is feeling. As discussed in the body language chapter, mirroring can help to put a person at ease by sending a voiceless signal that you're in harmony.

ACTION STEPS

On a conscious level communication is composed of talking, listening, and responding. Strike a balance between these actions. It may seem unnatural at first, especially if you're used to taking a listening mode. With practice, though, the idea is to increasingly bring a sense of levity to the affair, to inject more fun into dating. Taking more control of how you are in a conversation also leads to an enhanced sense of pride about the result of the encounter based on your active participation.

Ask questions that elicit interesting information. If you don't want to find yourself faced with a "yes" man or a "no" woman, be sure to ask questions that need more than one syllable to answer. Yes and no questions create a kind of start-and-stop dynamic. Just as you try to get the small talking going, you ask a question that goes nowhere. Open-ended questions require full answers, at least one sentence long. This gives the questioner fuel for the next question or to relate the answer back to his- or herself. Smooth conversation flows like a river that progresses around bends, picks up momentum, slows down in places, and passes fascinating scenery. Halting conversation keeps on drying up.

Review the comparison of questions later in this chapter. In one column are questions that can be answered with a yes or a no. The other column lists questions that require the respondent to elaborate.

One way of questioning leads to a nice long conversation that seems to fly by, while the other goes by painfully slow, sucking all the energy and oxygen out of the space around you.

THE EAR-LINK
Listen at least as much as you talk. Some experts recommend listening twice as much as you talk. Use these as guidelines. Try to stay flexible to the dynamics of your encounter and respond appropriately to the specifics of your date. If you're

being asked about yourself and you keep cutting your answers short in the name of politeness, you may interrupt the natural flow and exchange of conversation. Remember, both of you are hoping to hear information that gives real insight into the other person. You're trying to determine commonalities as well as tune into the unique chapters of another person's life. And, eliciting good information naturally provides an opening for us to relate back our own life experiences and interests.

Listen with real interest to what people have to say. Respond in a way that confirms you are listening. And, try to respond to the best individual aspects of a person.

SHARE TO ADVANCE

Don't squander how much you share about yourself. Letting someone else disclose personal details without sharing your own leaves them feeling a little naked. Some people may be timid and need a little more prodding to open up. But beware people who get you to talk about yourself without giving away any details about themselves. They may do this to retain what they perceive as "the power" in the interaction. If you sense this happening, ask one or two more direct questions about them. If you still aren't seeing a willingness to open up, then make a quick getaway. You're being played.

SHOW AND TELL AND DEVELOPING INTEREST

The weather, the location, the people in the room, and the food you are eating are all safe topics for conversation on a date. Yet, beyond the immediate stimuli available to spice up a tête-à-tête there are some additional ways to up your fascination quotient and to make your date feel likewise engaging. Remember, good energy is contagious and a bad attitude is deadly. If you feel like an interesting human you'll put across a sunnier outlook.

Knowledge is an awfully useful asset on a date. Make an effort to be informed or conversant on a diverse range of topics. This should reduce your own tension in unfamiliar social situations and help you to be perceived as a likeable and well-rounded person.

LEARN THE BASICS

If you have a specific "type" of person you'd like to attract or that you have a date with—such as a Wall Street investor, an actor, teacher, or a doctor—bone up on information about their job or be prepared with questions related to the work.

READ A NEWSPAPER OR GET NEWS ONLINE

Having a basic understanding about high-profile persons in a variety of fields broadens your conversational finesse. Read up on current social, literary/artistic, political, business, and cultural events that can enable you to reply to a range of questions and to spark conversations based on "Did you hear . . . ?" type comments. Know what's going on in your town and who is making an impact (the hottest restaurateur, local activist, or emerging political figure, etc.).

WATCH TELEVISION

While watching too much television can cause voids in your personal activity profile, some viewing can be helpful for tuning into popular culture.

TAKE A CLASS

Night classes and weekend seminars are readily available in most communities. Diverse class topics abound. Not only will you enrich your daily life, you'll be more interesting and have more topics to discuss. You may even find that your new skill will enable you to help someone out with a particular issue or problem they are having in one of these areas.

EMULATE GOOD CONVERSATIONALISTS

Go hear interesting speakers. Watch talk show hosts like David Letterman, Ellen DeGeneres, and Jon Stewart. Read interviews in magazines that have a question-and-answer format. Interviews clearly show how to take the answer to one question and build on it with your next question. This format also provides examples for following an answer with a comment that reveals something about yourself. Good interviewers provide you with verbal examples of how to validate others and put them at ease.

RE-MEET YOURSELF

We think that we know ourselves, but how often do we stop to think specifically what it is that makes us unique and interesting? What combination of experiences, personality traits, talents, skills, and interests make you who you are?

Rewards for being a well-read and informed person are many. Potentially you may become a more involved person who has more dates and new friends, as a result of making easier connections with others. Being well informed can positively affect your career and community ties. At the very least, you'll become a more engaging person with lots to talk about.

A Question Companion

Questions that invite one-word answers	Questions that invite personal stories and facts
"Do you like jazz?"	"What is your favorite type of music/your favorite musician?"
"Is this your first time to this restaurant?"	"I've eaten here before and it's great. What types of food (or cuisine) do you enjoy?"
"Do you enjoy living in New York?"	"What brought you to New York?"
"So you're a chemist. Is that an interesting job?"	"I've never met a chemist before. What attracted you to that type of work (or the industry)?"
"Do you have any hobbies?"	"I've really gotten into wine tasting in the last year. What do you most enjoy doing in your spare time?"
"Does your family live in New York?"	"My family is 2,000 miles away in Florida and I don't get to see them as much as I'd like. Where does your family live?"

DATING DOS

The most straightforward goal of a date is to be engaging and likable. The other person wouldn't have agreed to the date if they weren't hoping to have an enjoyable time.

1. Be joyously confident or nervously confident. We each have something to offer by way of our company. Know that some of your essence will be glimpsed. And, keep in mind that, no one date can reflect your complete self.

2. Enjoy the process. There is nothing to fear because on a date you take one step (an opening question perhaps) and observe what happens, and then you decide on the next step. These introductory dating steps are necessary to take you to the next phase and next steps in a relationship.

3. Learn from the experience. All humans have good and negative experiences, especially when it comes to interacting with other human beings. As long as you learn from the experience, you're progressing.

4. Try to reveal something of yourself. A little mystery is good on a date, but you don't want your date struggling to figure you out either.

5. Take a break when you need to. This is what bathrooms are for. A few minutes can give you time to ponder your progress or to regroup.

6. Have positive expectations that a date will go well, but be open to the fact that a date, and a relationship, can play out in many different ways. It can begin differently than we imagined, and it can progress more quickly or slowly than we had planned. Don't let your need for one result deter-

mine your feelings about whether a date is worthwhile or a success.

7. Trust your instincts. Instincts can make you feel particularly "right" about someone: that they have a good heart, that you have a purpose in having met each other. Our instincts also tell us when something just doesn't seem right. If your instincts are screaming "run!" walk calmly to the nearest exit.

DATING DON'TS

To keep interaction moving along, much like traffic signs, knowing what not to do can often be as helpful as knowing the right things to do.

1. Don't always be "on." To cover nerves it is sometimes tempting to talk nonstop or to try out all our "best" lines and attention-getting tactics, one after the other. We shoot off a barrage of questions without waiting for answers. Some people even put on an alter ego (the belle of the ball, the jokester, the suave Frenchman, etc.) that takes over and won't step aside for the real you. After a while it feels awkward to go "natural," and your date is exhausted trying to relate to a real character.

2. Don't try too hard. This category includes being unnaturally polite, making sure there are absolutely no silences, laughing too often, using profane language, and being too intense or serious, to name a few common manifestations. If you find yourself doing these things, take a breath and relax. Use the pause to think of something you'd really like

to know about the person or to comment on an observation you've made during the pause. You can even comment on people's lack of comfort during silence.

3. Don't lie to impress your date. You don't want to have to cover your tracks later because you said you had a better job position than you do, more important responsibilities, a higher salary, a famous friend/acquaintance, or the perfect family. These kinds of things are better left as a discussion about your hopes or goals for the future.

4. Don't keep your date waiting. No matter how wonderful you look by taking all that extra time to get ready, it's not polite to keep a date waiting or worrying whether they got the right time or place.

5. Don't overcompliment. Everyone enjoys a sincere compliment. "You have a lovely smile," "You have beautiful eyes," "What a great laugh," "You seem very intelligent," "What a generous thing to do for your family." If your date starts to squirm or looks uneasy, you've gone overboard with the compliments or got too personal (some personal remarks that are too body specific have all the finesse of a sledgehammer).

6. Don't jump to conclusions or make immediate judgments. Lack of confidence or personal history can cause us to be oversensitive. A date is a time of exploration. Make sure that you are leaving yourself open to really hearing, and are allowing your date to speak for him or herself (rather than you silently filling in the blanks or making inferences). If you are unsure about something that is said, ask for clarification or ask a question that gives you more information.

7. Don't forecast failure. You create what you imagine. Practice feeling confident—that you have unique insights, information, life experiences, personal qualities, viewpoints, and emotional energy to share.

CHAPTER 5

Everyday Mingling

The importance of developing a sense of play about socializing and cultivating curiosity about your neighbors was previously touched upon, but now let's explore this area at more length. Why? Because your community and neighbors offer a plethora of opportunities to increase your small talk and social savvy through enjoyable practice, while also making you feel more connected to the people around you. Within blocks of your home, apartment, or condo you'll find a wealth of chances to enlarge your circle of friends and support network, as well as grow your pool of potential romantic partners. Recently I heard a radio deejay state that if you date approximately one third of the available people you know, you're very likely to connect with Mr. or Ms. Right. I would think that having a diverse group of people to select from would greatly enhance the enjoyment of this process.

EXTENDING YOURSELF AROUND THE NEIGHBORHOOD

As we discussed in Chapters 2 and 3, planning, attitude, and attention play major roles in how successfully you interact with others. Small talk savvy becomes second nature only after positive intentions are enacted repeatedly. Yet, modern life offers up many distractions to our best social intentions—both of our own making and stemming from collective community mindsets. Keep aware of potential communication roadblocks in order to limit their effect on your social success. Common hindrances to improved face-to-face communication, to name a few, include:

- Being an electronic junkie—how long can you go without using your cell phone?
- Work overload and life overscheduling—you know who you are.
- A standoffish community personality—pervasive communal attitudes can affect ease of interaction.
- Living independent minded—modern living often supports the notion of the rugged individualist: each man or woman as a soloist in day-to-day living.
- Assumptions about commonalities and differences—coming to conclusions based on what we see rather than what we know about a given individual.

You can't change other people, but you can be more open yourself and show another way of being. Even subtle changes in your approach to people—exhibiting your belief in the pleasure of a friendly hello and in the value of getting to know people—can go far in creating positive results. Recognize that there is a richness of human connection waiting to be tapped. Just be sure you're not throwing up roadblocks that are within your control to get past or eliminate.

POTENTIAL ROADBLOCK ONE: BEING AN ELECTRONIC JUNKIE

So, how socially connected are you? You may have a computer and access to the Internet, a cell phone, and an instant messaging device and may still not be optimally connecting with the people around you. While electronics have made daily life convenient in many ways, these gadgets haven't exactly made us more apt to notice our fellow humans.

There's a social downside to communicating in speed dial mode all the time. We can get out of practice with (or never become familiar with) engaging in focused and meaningful interactions up close and personal. For many of us there are fewer quiet spaces ("Can you hear me?") throughout the day for being in touch with what's going on around us. The following exercises are designed to help you recognize the opportunities for more neighborly connections, as well as help set the stage for the subsequent small talk opportunities that can arise from simple states of awareness and friendliness.

MODERN COMMUNICATIONS—A TRUE-OR-FALSE QUIZ

1. A busy life equals a life of substance.
2. Constant cell phone use or instant messaging confers an air of importance or popularity upon the user.
3. Electronics keep people well connected.
4. If I'm not available 24/7, I'll miss an important opportunity.

ANSWERS

1. False. Busy can have "meat" to it or not. Some busyness is disorganized tail chasing; some is the result of needlessly overextending ourselves; some of us create an inordinate amount of activity to cover for a less than thrilling, fulfilling, or balanced existence (workaholics use this one).

2. False. True electronics give you quick access to others, but since nearly everyone has a cell phone or other communication device these days, the cachet it once had is a thing of the past. Beware of cell phone abuse—talking on the phone anywhere without discrimination or consideration of others. It is not only impolite, it can be perceived as your discomfort with your own company. Any handheld communication device used in public reduces your big picture awareness of what is going on around you.

3. It depends. Electronics keep you connected. Whether or not you are well connected is up to you. Well connected is using electronics to stay in touch more often with people you wouldn't otherwise (because you just weren't a letter writer, etc.), or to be more considerate to others (you can call if you'll be late or to inform about your whereabouts). Well connected is employing electronics to reach a greater number of potential business contacts. On the other hand, you are probably not well connected if you use communication devices as a personal shield or distancing device (so you don't have to talk to people, so people won't approach you or ask you questions, etc.), as your primary form of entertainment, or instead of human-to-human contact.

4. In most cases, false. Hardly anyone is so important that a message won't suffice. Over-reliance on always being

"available" may be giving you a false sense of importance. Others could see this as you using your communication devices as a personality or confidence prop. If you can't leave the house or the office without your cell phone ever, reconsider being such a satellite slave.

SOCIAL SKILL BUILDING EXERCISE #1:
SWITCHING TO OBSERVATION MODE

The next time you run errands, turn off your cell phone. Make a point of watching how other people are interacting with one another. Is there more politeness or curtness? Are people engaged in more than one activity at a time? Who seems to be having the most positive interactions? Did you see anyone with whom you would have liked to have a chat?

SOCIAL SKILL BUILDING EXERCISE #2:
FACING THE WORLD WITH A SMILE

Be the smiling face in the crowd. Smile and make eye contact with people you pass on the sidewalk, smile at the person in the car next to you when you are stopped at a light, smile at other shoppers in the grocery aisle or at the mall. Note the reactions of other people. Were they pleasantly surprised? Did they warmly return the smile, or say hello? Who was afraid to meet your glance or outright ignored you? Notice how an abundance of smiling makes you feel.

POTENTIAL ROADBLOCK TWO:
WORK OVERLOAD AND LIFE OVERSCHEDULING

With all the layoffs and downsizing that have taken place in the last decade it's not uncommon for an employee to be doing the job of two people. Everyone has gotten used to doing more as vacant positions remain unfilled and seasonally heavy workloads become a full time reality. We're busy and pressed for time, which can mean less relating to people in a warm, interested, and caring way that is mutually supportive of meaningful interaction.

In addition, some people have gotten onto the "I'm just so busy" treadmill. No matter when you call or talk with them they are running off to do something "really" important or they have another fire to put out. There is a difference between hectic and satisfying. Don't fall into the trap of creating noise in your life that doesn't feed your basic need for real connections. In even the busiest schedule, room can be made for a few minutes of friendly chitchat. A little small talk can really brighten your outlook on an otherwise hectic day.

SOCIAL SKILL BUILDING EXERCISE #3: STEPPING OUT BY ACTING ON INTEREST

Be aware of who interests you in your building, on your street, or in your town. Make an intention to introduce yourself and find out a bit about them. Then follow through. For instance, want to know if that rather attractive someone down the hall is attached? Plan to ask them how they like living in the building the next time you run into them taking out the trash, working out in the building gym, or going to their car. Want to take it a step beyond? Mention how you're so busy that you haven't had a chance to meet many people, but that you were thinking of having a cocktail party soon to remedy that situation. Do they know people in the building who might like a social get-together? Direct small talk can effectively get you information you can act on to create new social opportunities.

SOCIAL SKILL BUILDING EXERCISE #4:
GIFTING OTHERS WITH GOOD PRESENCE

Commit to giving your attention to those you interact with, even if it's only for two minutes. Create the intention to be friendly and polite to people you normally engage rather mindlessly. Ask how their day is going or comment on their job or service. This exercise is intended to provide practice for being fully present and sincere, which is a great way to begin any interaction. Practicing with effective quick interactions helps to make you more relaxed with exchanges of additional length and depth.

POTENTIAL ROADBLOCK THREE:
A STANDOFFISH COMMUNITY PERSONALITY

Each community, town, and city has its own general personality that may make connecting and interacting with others a challenge. For instance, some gated communities don't seem particularly conducive to intermingling. Commuting suburbs often present the problem of people going to and from their respective homes right into their various modes of transportation with absolutely no interaction with neighbors. People living in cities can become so self-sufficient that asking a neighbor for the proverbial cup of sugar would be unthinkable. The suburbs present their own challenges. One friend bemoaned the fact that she moved into an established neighborhood pretty much closed to the idea of making new acquaintances—the equivalent of a closed circle of people at a party. Sometimes you may have to search out more obviously friendly contacts than your next-door neighbor, but first determine whether any perceived attitude is fixed or flexible.

SOCIAL SKILL BUILDING EXERCISE #5:
SPARKING QUICK CONNECTIONS

Practice noticing and finding connections. If you're a commuter your best connection time may be on trains, subways, buses, or in taxis. Talk with your co-commuters. Comment on their reading materials or ask for assistance on a crossword puzzle word. Again, the weather is always an easy opener. Use the time to practice your small talk skills. Taxi drivers are nearly always from somewhere else, so ask where they hail from. Who have you noticed before that you might want to get to know? Take advantage of community events and scheduled get-togethers like condominium pool parties or neighborhood farmers' markets and art walks. People who live near you frequent such events and are there for a common purpose. Even an unscheduled occurrence like an apartment electrical outage can create a neighbor-bonding framework. When I lived in Philadelphia I met all the neighbors on my apartment floor during one of the many outages in our building. I could have stayed in my apartment but it seemed like more fun to go out in the hall where people were chatting, laughing, and exchanging candles.

SOCIAL SKILL BUILDING EXERCISE #6:
CONNECTING WITH PERSONAL STYLE

Are you on friendly terms with the people you interact with on a regular basis—the dry cleaner, the bank teller, the tailor, the post office clerks, or the waiters or waitresses at your favorite restaurant? My remedy for living in a big "impersonal" city and working at home was to get my social interaction fix talking with local shop owners. Make it a point to explore your neighborhood.

You Can Meet People in the Most Mundane Places

Everyday haunts make good places to meet people because you're likely to see the same people time after time if you're paying attention. Playfully investigate and be willing to initiate conversation.

POTENTIAL ROADBLOCK FOUR: LIVING INDEPENDENT MINDED

Maybe it's those old reruns of *Dick Van Dyke* and *I Dream of Jeannie*, but it seems like generations past connected more often with their neighbors, coworkers, and community members. They seemed open to coming together on a regular basis for community welfare and social entertainment. Generations past joined the local country club and fraternal organizations like the Elks Club. They played bridge and pinochle, and invited neighbors to join them for barbecues and cocktails on the patio.

Today, in general, we're a much more independent lot and much busier to boot. When was the last time you asked your neighbor for assistance with something or spontaneously invited them to spend time with you? These days if a neighbor does something extraordinarily kind it's apt to make the local news. And, there are fewer rules about traditional roles and the timing of our life endeavors, so we're not always in sync with our neighbors in our career and relationship phases.

Establishing connections that enrich your life may take a bit more concerted effort. This could mean joining a book club, alumni group, adult softball or soccer league, a weekend running or bike club, local charity or environmental cause, or a single parents group. Perhaps you and a friend could turn a fledging interest into a group dynamic—work together to establish a regular dining club (eating out or taking turns making themed dinners in) or a wine tasting group. This creates a regular basis for getting together, and for meeting new people as new members join. The great thing about joining a specific group is that you immediately have something in common to small talk about, and the repetition provides a natural schedule for establishing, nurturing, and growing relationships.

SOCIAL SKILL BUILDING EXERCISE #7: INVITING INTERACTION

Create an interactive event. This may be a garage sale, house-warming, themed holiday party, or casual cocktail soiree—anything that brings people from your community to your door. You might make a great lifelong friend or you may meet someone who provides another kind of valuable life connection—such as a great masseuse or an investment adviser. Holidays make a good time to invite neighbors over for holiday cheer. Be sure to follow up with your new connections to determine who is open to continuing a relationship. Asking people to join you for coffee, to walk dogs together, or to exercise (jog, walk, play tennis, or take an exercise class), if you know they engage in such activities, is a reasonable next stage activity.

SOCIAL SKILL BUILDING EXERCISE #8:
STIMULATING DÉJÀ VU ASSOCIATIONS

Join a repeat event like the annual garden tour, a benefit golf tournament, run/walk for cancer research, or an annual arts or music related event. This provides a structure for building a history with a particular group of people. People will remember your participation from year to year, and you open yourself to the possibility of extending particular relationships beyond the event. For instance, you could suggest to people who volunteer and work hard for a charity event that they reward themselves afterward by visiting a local spa together.

POTENTIAL ROADBLOCK FIVE:
ASSUMPTIONS ABOUT COMMONALITIES AND DIFFERENCES

Sometimes our assumptions about what we have in common with certain people restrict our openness to new encounters. Our assumptions may be based on age, culture, appearance, or lifestyle. Stay open-minded with an open heart. Small encounters like these marvelously layer and "fill in the gaps" of our existence. They can create a cumulative sense of fullness. Be receptive to overtures by others and initiate your own.

SOCIAL SKILL BUILDING EXERCISE #9:
COMPLIMENTARY CONNECTIONS

Make a point of speaking with people of all ages, from the kids fidgeting in line at the post office to the older folks in the grocery store. Asking for others' opinions (on clothes, food, gifts, etc.) is a good way to engage someone in a little affable dialogue. Offering assistance or being complimentary can also make someone's day. "Love that shirt. It looks great on you." "Beautiful necklace, where did you get it?" It's like giving an unexpected gift. Good energy is contagious, so do your part to generously generate it.

SOCIAL SKILL BUILDING EXERCISE #10: OPEN ARMS

Keep aware of new neighbors moving in. Be timely (within the first couple of weeks) about stopping by to introduce yourself and to welcome them to the apartment building/condo complex/neighborhood. Take a thoughtful or helpful gift. A list of neighbors' names with addresses and phone numbers is a friendly gesture, as is providing a list of your favorite restaurants and reliable vendors such as electrician, handyman, and plumber.

Your social universe expands proportionately to the energy that you expend. Don't overthink social encounters, rather strive to be the friendly face that walks into a store, and the smiling face that says "hello" on the street. Make time to chat with neighbors. Get comfortable in not knowing or having expectations about where a conversation will lead. By putting yourself out there, by being the "approachable" person in a crowd, your satisfying people connections are bound to grow.

ADVANCING YOUR LOVE OF CONVERSATION

Often we get into a rut about with whom, when, and where we communicate. Try stretching beyond habit and comfort zone. Make little small talk strides that enliven your days and enlarge your social world. So often people just need someone else to brave the first word, to make the first move. Be that someone and see what a difference it makes in how you perceive your communication abilities:

At the grocery store. Why waste a good wait in line with silence? Survey what the person in front or back of you has in their cart or up on the counter. Try a friendly, "Looks like you're having pasta for dinner," "You look like you're having a party," or "I'm impressed you eat so healthy."

In the elevator. Ah elevators, the land of the blank stare and uneasy space shifting. Yet there is small talk lurking there. Getting on the elevator you might comment, "Thanks for holding the elevator, it took me so long to get here this morning, what terrible traffic." Since everyone is in such close quarters it usually takes just one person to make a first move that relaxes the entire group.

Around the home and garden. Bridge that lawn gap by proactively commenting on your neighbor's new plants, obvious green thumb or golf-course perfect lawn when you're outdoors at the same time. If they have a little remodeling work going on, ask how it's proceeding. Volunteer to water their lawn when they go on vacation or ask if you can leave your house key with them while you are on vacation in case of emergencies. This creates opportunities for establishing trust.

At the gym. Health clubs can be favorable places to meet people, but use common sense about initiating exchanges. Rather than talking to the treadmill runner, head to the stationary bikes for conversation. People tend to be less out of breath and even read while riding. Ask someone on a machine or lifting weights how much longer they'll be or how many more reps they have (in as friendly a not-rushing-you manner as you can). This can lead to a comment about the obvious results of their workout or your discomfort (you're not sure you're using it correctly) with the particular machine. (Don't take it personally if certain individuals don't engage you. For some, workouts are serious self-concentrated time.)

CHAPTER 6

Nourishing Small Talk: Home Entertaining and Business Meals

You've done the bar scene, you've dated, and you're getting to know your neighbors. Still, you haven't quite perfected the more formal socializing bit. The more structured nature of a sit-down event may make you feel a little out of your element. It's true, taking part in a meal with a small group of diners makes for an intimate dining experience. It demands slightly different actions from both hosts and guests. In this social or business situation you won't be roaming once you begin a meal, so no escaping the deadly bore. But you can use your small talk skills to allay "performance" anxiety and to find the fun in each situation. These happenings present splendid opportunities for you to meet a diverse range of people and for colleagues and clients to further glimpse your winning personality.

SOCIALIZING AT SIT-DOWN DINNERS AND LUNCHEONS

There is no better way to get to know a few people than over a meal. Dinner parties and luncheons create an immediately intimate environment conducive to forming affable bonds with others. The mere act of being in close contact with other people, sitting next to one another, invites closeness both physical and emotional. And, in many cases these meals present the chance to meet people you might not otherwise know were it not for a host creating a stage: a specific setting, time, and place for the introduction.

Sit-down can also mean an annual buffet bash that brings together your divergent group of friends from the different areas of your life: work, childhood and school friends, charity work, sports or exercise partners, new acquaintances, and current friends. Seasonal dinner parties are great for socializing with people you either don't normally have the time to have over for dinner or acquaintances you want to keep in friendly contact with, but don't necessarily want to make a close buddy. Sharing a meal with others is an especially ideal climate in which to maintain and grow relationships, work or personal. Lunches are more low pressure than dinners when you'd like to casually get to know someone better, either on a romantic or friendly basis.

Don't shy away from a potentially jovial way to socialize that gives you a great deal of control. As a host you control factors such as the guest list, the menu, the tone (dressed up or casual), and the entertainment. Done well, inviting people to your table is the perfect way to share a satisfying good time.

THE INVITE

Socially speaking: Joyce, a hostess extraordinaire for decades, has been known to have three cocktail parties in one weekend. Asked the secret to her social success, she emphatically says that if you want to meet people just ask them! "I genuinely like people, and everyone seems to enjoy being invited to socialize. Also, I often make the first move. If you're friendly, look people in the eye and smile, they are very receptive." Grab opportunities as they arise and be direct and sincere: "I'd love to have you over to dinner," or "I'm so happy to have met you. Would you like to join me for lunch this week?" For dinner parties of twelve or fewer, a verbal invite is generally fine. If it's a special occasion like a birthday or some type of congratulations celebration, consider an invitation that clearly states the reason for the gathering. And, of course, written invitations, with RSVP information, help you to organize larger gatherings. For a dinner party with a theme and/or dress guidelines a written invitation reinforces the theme from the onset, and helps to get people into the spirit of the affair. If the guests will be requested to participate in any activity other than dining, a written invitation helps to spell that out. Mailed invitations are more personal (and less likely to get deleted or tossed in the junk mail bin), but email is increasingly being used for invitations. Use common sense and the format that you know works best for contacting your particular invitees.

Business-wise: Informal business luncheons and business dinners often spring spontaneously from groups of people attending the same business conference or event. Verbal invitations are extended. At times employees are verbally requested or required to attend luncheons or dinners in which the company has purchased a table for a specific event. Business events requesting the attendance of nonemployees are usually handled with a written invitation explaining the reason for the gathering: the launch of a new product, a press conference, a company anniversary, a groundbreaking, and so on. In addition to the standard date, time, and place, the invitation should outline the activities taking place, mention any guest(s) of honor in attendance, and include the names of any officials/persons making presentations. Most businesspeople have numerous demands made on their time, so make sure that they have the facts they need to make an informed choice about attendance.

Business meetings and events are not about surprises; it's about putting attendees in an optimal frame of mind for participation and interaction.

THE ARRIVAL AND INTRODUCTIONS

Socially speaking: Once someone is at your home, making the person feel welcomed is key to his or her comfort level. Showing someone around your home or apartment is a nice welcoming gesture. It communicates that you have opened your doors to their company. And, of course, introducing them to other guests helps to minimize initial mingling awkwardness. Introduce guests by stating their names and one or two interesting things about them: "This is Sally Jones, a good friend from high school and an amazing interior designer." "This is my neighbor John Smith. He just started his doctorate in Civil War history." This immediately gives people topics for conversation, such as what style of interior design they favor, or how long they've lived next door.

As a guest, you can launch small talk by saying something appropriately complimentary to your host like: "Lovely food," or "It smells good in here." If the home has been specially decorated for the dinner, comment on it: "Beautiful Christmas tree." Bringing something more imaginative than flowers or a bottle of wine as a host/hostess gift can make you memorable, and give you something to talk about right away. Use good judgment here. An exotic plant, selection of fine teas, or unique coaster set reflects out-of-the-box thinking. Avoid kitschy gifts (like porcine salt and pepper shakers), and sports or holiday-themed items, since these are so specific to individual tastes.

If you know that you'll be attending a luncheon or dinner in which you won't know the other guests, you can plan (or volunteer) to be one of the first to arrive so that you can offer the hostess assistance. Offer to open champagne or to finish setting up the buffet. This tactic enables you to make yourself helpful and to be in a position to meet everyone as they arrive. Just don't be so early that the hostess is annoyed rather than grateful. Ask guests how they know the hostess or other guests. Observe the interaction as you listen so that you get a sense of people's commonalities and how they are connected. Do a number of people belong to the same needlepoint club or go to the same gym? There almost always will be someone in the group who will be warm and welcoming to a guest outside the regular group.

Business-wise: Business gatherings of either all coworkers or people from a mix of companies and businesses offer built-in small talk fodder. Topics you can discuss to create a comfortable atmosphere include the following.

- Architecture (if you or the other guests are from out of town, local landmarks make a good topic)
- Food and wine
- Traffic/weather
- Travel experiences
- City/country of origin
- Current events/info in the news
- How long someone has been with a company
- What do they think of the current industry direction or competitive companies
- Who really impresses them at their company or who do they think is a businessperson of note
- How they got into the industry
- An important pending company or industry event (such as a company going public or an industry conference)

If you have trouble remembering information you hear, try taking notes after a dinner or lunch. When you get back to your desk or arrive home, make notations about the particular interests of certain people, current life happenings, the names of family members, anniversary dates, and so on. You can use the information later to refresh your acquaintance by asking questions related to the information such as, "Didn't you close on your new home last week?" "How did your son's hockey game go?" "Have you been able to get out and enjoy your new boat?" Again, use small talk as a valuable relationship tool that strengthens initial connections.

THE ENERGY/ENTERTAINMENT

Socially speaking: It greases the wheels of small talk to have the "energy" of the event emanate from a focused source initially. This might be the hostess who makes the introductions and who sets the tone for interaction. It may be a guest of honor to whom everyone wants to say hello. Event themes enhance energy at a luncheon or dinner by injecting an aura of celebration or an invitation to step outside normal day-to-day behavior. A hired entertainer (piano player, jazz ensemble, strolling minstrels, cabaret performer, or comedian) can create energy that gets everyone talking. Games go well with backyard meals. Break out the bocce balls, horseshoes, archery, croquet, or volleyball set to generate excitement and break down any personality or social barriers.

Business-wise: At a business meal, the social energy may be generated by the most important person at the event, such as the company president or CEO, who establishes the tone and topics for interaction. In many cases head honchos are looking for a moment to relax and may prefer that everyone carry their own social weight, so to speak. Being aware of the dynamic that exists can be crucial to interaction ease. If you want to single out someone (who is not at your table) for contact, do it between courses or following the meal. Make it brief. For instance, thank the company president for putting on a great event. At a Christmas dinner you might find an opportunity to say something like: "Thank you for the wonderful evening. I'm excited about business for the coming year."

At a business event with the purpose of conveying information—whether it's a press conference or a business-specific presentation—that action takes center stage (usually at the beginning of the event) and becomes the source for initial conversation once food is served. If a restaurant meal is really a working session rather than a cordial sharing of food and thoughts, then that is the focus throughout the gathering. Everything else, including the food, is secondary. Make a menu selection quickly and get on with business.

As is true for any social affair, business gatherings bring together a variety of personality types. It usually takes some effort on each participant's part to contribute to the flow of conversation. Plan to be proactive about your participation. Business can be pleasure with an upbeat attitude, good manners, and the skills to ignite a little conversational spark.

Party Icebreakers

Party icebreakers enliven parties and provide an excuse for anyone and everyone to intermingle. Try this idea:

Master the Prop—The host/hostess provides various props to guests as they arrive: monocles, fake cigar/cigarette, feather boa, cane, fake mustache, funky hat, belt (Western or sumo), and so on. This gives people a reason to speak to anyone; they have a license to get engaged lightheartedly with one another.

THE MEAL

Socially speaking: There is a degree of truth that who you sit next to determines your enjoyment of a meal. But, just remember that everyone is thinking just that, so strive to be the interesting conversationalist and good listener that is a pleasure to be seated next to. At dinners the hostess usually determines who sits next to whom. If she or he (or you) does a good job at seating placements you should have someone with a similar background or perhaps an entirely different life experience to speak with and get to know. You have people on either side of you so strive to balance your communications with both sides. Perhaps speak with one person early in the meal and turn your attention to the second person during dessert and coffee. Sometimes the flow of conversations from one side to the next flows naturally. At times a topic will engage the entire table. Some hostesses like to have diners switch seats with each course to enable people to mingle even as they dine. The only time you may want to sit quietly is when you are listening for a natural place to enter a new conversation. Otherwise use your small talk skills to draw others out and to reveal aspects of yourself.

Eating too quickly, overconsuming alcohol, splaying your elbows on the table, and using a boardinghouse reach are common faux pas. If you're not sure about proper etiquette or table manners in a range of situations, consider doing the following:

- Take a class to refresh yourself.
- Purchase a book and practice being genteel with friends.
- Review the basics online before your next business trip.

Manners are part of the script for putting yourself at ease in social situations and for showing respect to your host.

Business-wise: For a large percentage of sit-down dinners and luncheons you'll either select from the menu or someone else has made the choice for you. On occasion you may have the job of selecting the restaurant. Steakhouses are a perennial favorite with the traditional business crowd, but try to know the tastes of the most senior person at a dinner. They may be a more adventurous diner or happy to break from the routine. If you know you'll be out of town, do research on the Internet to find out about reputable restaurants or hot new dining finds. Then you'll be able to make good recommendations while everyone else is mumbling about not knowing what's around. When you take people out for a meal, you are essentially the host or hostess so be conscientious about that role. If the meal is definitely all business, be sure your guests are satisfied with their menu options but don't be too distracted by the food yourself. This type of meal is more about creating a forum for discussing some specific business issue.

In the business world, differentiation is good. This concept can extend through every aspect of business including the meal. Context is important in all effective communication, so consider factors such as what do you know about the people who will be in attendance? How important is food to the success of the event? Many event organizers play it "safe" with dull menu choices, which really reflects their inattentiveness to the importance of food and/or wanting to please everyone—a weak strategy. In both pleasure and business it is impossible to please everyone, especially when it comes to food—thanks to diets from hell, and food sensitivities. (Generally, I don't believe in catering to the tastes of picky or nonadventurous eaters over the age of ten.) You can't know all the food peculiarities, so aim to create a memorable dinner or luncheon in which the food is a key ingredient that whets the appetite for insightful and fascinating conversation. Don't overstress about it, but do take some care in choosing a restaurant or in planning a meal. A good meal nourishes social intercourse.

FOLLOWING UP AND REINFORCING CONNECTIONS

Always send a thank-you note to your host or hostess. Keep it simple. Mention the aspects of the meal or gathering that stood out to you: the food, the atmosphere, or the entertainment. You can thank the host for introducing you to a particular person whose company you especially enjoyed. If a colleague arranged an event, send a brief email expressing appreciation. It also makes good sense to send thank-you notes to potential business partners or clients following an initial meeting. They should not only express your thanks for the person(s) taking the time to meet with you, but also include your next action step: "I will be calling you next week to continue our discussion."

Relationships die when they aren't attended to. So be creative with how you want to keep a connection alive. It's a nice personal touch to follow up a particularly good interaction with an article or news clipping that relates to a subject of interest that was discussed or touched upon. It shows that you were truly interested and that you would like to grow the connection. For instance, if someone you spoke with mentioned that they just got a new golden retriever and you run across an article about the heroic deeds of dogs you could forward it with a brief note, "I enjoyed meeting you Saturday night. Being in puppy love heaven, I thought you would find this article interesting about what you have to look forward to." It could be an article about a red wine find, or describing a hot new dining spot or retail shop. The busier everyone gets, the more the little touches mean. Be a standout socializer from beginning to end.

PERSONAL ASSETS THAT RULE

In all these social situations the right attitude goes far. Have a sense of humor. It's a social event, not a job review. Make levity your life preserver. Humorous self-deprecating comments and disarming remarks usually merit positive response. Donna, a Wilmington, Delaware, marketing executive, relates that a guy once asked her, "Didn't I have chicken at your house once?" Her mother had asked so many people over to dinner over the years that she actually paused to think about it before realizing that he was kidding. She relates, "It seems like a pretty silly line, but its ridiculousness made me laugh." Don't underestimate the charm and tension-relieving power of a little humor.

Empathy and compassion go far in social and business situations. You can take an active role in every social endeavor. In fact, action gives you a sense of control. If you feel like you need rescuing, rescue someone else instead. Who do you see alone that would appreciate your coming to his aid? Approach him with a smile and say, "Hi, I'm . . . I don't know anyone and am feeling a little awkward. What is your name?" Engage children if they are present—no one feels weirder than them probably. Embrace your own kind presence as an asset and people will discern an attractive nature.

Whether it's a strictly social affair or a business-oriented coming together, people respond positively to the same basic cues: a genuine smile, a connected gaze, and a warm handshake. Want to be seen as really amiable and attractive? Fully participate and be upbeat. Make others feel comfortable interacting with you and the reflected glow will put you in a good light. One of my all-time favorite lines is from the movie *Auntie Mame*. Rosalind

Russell, playing the epitome of an erudite, open-minded, and lively socializer, states her motto of living a highly engaged life: "Life is a banquet, and most poor suckers are starving to death!" The ability to carry on small talk should prevent you from ever going home from a dinner party hungry for good conversation. Everyone has something interesting about them; use small talk and open-ended questions to find out just what. Make sure that you get your fill of new personalities and fascinating stories. Your life and business relationships will be richer for it.

CHAPTER 7

Small Talk Muscle in the Workplace

Good news! All the small talk skills that you acquire in your social interactions aptly translate to successful work interactions, with a few modifications. Small talk is a universal language that can be employed for improved and supportive coworker relationships, more effective exchanges with bosses and superiors, and greater ease with clients and customers.

The workplace provides you with natural conversation topics and built-in frameworks, such as informal and scheduled meetings. You are in the right place at the right time because you have a purpose. Fears about interaction should thus be minimized; you were invited into the group. Yet, many people feel pressure to "perform" at work. Some of this is about work contributions and part of this is about wanting to be perceived in a particular "right" way. Various workplace environments have different dynamics and share many common traits. Principles such as a positive attitude, awareness of your surroundings, a confident physical presence, conversation know-how, and respectful listening can take you far. Implement your small talk skills by:

- Using your observation skills to get to know workplace dynamics.
- Being yourself. You shouldn't have to be a different person to succeed. Know how to work your strengths and when to build up desirable traits.
- Reducing fears or uncertainties with positive action. Engaging in actions that fulfill work responsibilities (helping you to be perceived as reliable), or that contribute to the team effort.
- Engaging in professional interactions that are genuinely friendly, respectful, and fruitful.
- Emulating success (another form of mirroring).

Press the Dress

"Press the dress" refers to staying on top of guidelines, sometimes unspoken, for self-presentation in various work circumstances in order to harmonize your professional know-how with expected standards for appearance. Select apparel that best suits the working impression you want to create so that you will be at ease and at your best. Basics for proper dress in the workplace include:

- Know the code. Whether it is at your place of work or at the offices of a client, know what type of dress is appropriate. Dress codes vary significantly.
- Colors communicate. Be aware of the effects certain colors will have on others. For example, red is a high-energy and socially strong color.
- Avoid extremes. Stay away from too short, too tight, too busy, too many ruffles, too much jewelry, worn out, or decidedly passé.

MINGLING MOJO AND BUSINESS STRATA

Work mingling is multistratum socializing. You are chatting with your coworker one moment, meeting with a client the next, and reporting to your boss after that. Each interaction, successfully done, requires subtle shifts in WHAT you relate and HOW you relate it. Talking with a coworker probably does not have a strict timeframe, while speaking with a boss may be extremely time sensitive, both in terms of bringing her attention to a matter affecting a project in the works, and in terms of how long you spend imparting the information. Putting a potential client at ease helps to set the stage for receptivity to what you have to say, while a busy superior may want you to take a more direct approach in your communication. Being in tune with these dynamics as you interact gives you natural cues for how to approach and conduct your communication.

BOSS CONTACT

Like everyone else, bosses want to be put at ease. They appreciate optimism. Traits like preparedness (for meetings, for presentations, etc.), decisiveness, taking responsibility for actions, and being reliable are generally regarded well by superiors. If you do your job well, then interacting should not be hugely intimidating. Your boss should have only good feelings about your presence and participation.

Remember communication is the exchange of information, and bosses love to be kept informed of what's happening, both good and bad. This provides employees with an ideal reason to instigate communication with a superior (following the appropriate channels for communication, of course). Timing plays a role in the positive exchange of work updates, especially if something has changed. Be proactive and responsible. For instance, you might initiate a conversation with, "Do you have a minute? I just wanted to give you an update on the Best Life project." Or you may want to highlight a work success that you are privy to: "Everything is going great with the Best Life project. I met with the client today and they expressed how happy they are with the hard work they're seeing on the ad campaign." Constructive communication includes making sure that your boss doesn't get surprised by a work development. Use a calm manner or tone and be organized with your thoughts when addressing work challenges. In general, be positive in your communications. Rather than telling a boss why you can't do something, let them know how you can.

In work situations, it's not unusual for employees who are interacting with a superior to use impressing tactics such as bragging about what they do or about what they have. Yet, a better tactic is to aim to put people at ease. It's effective even with the bigwigs. Ask questions that are more down-to-earth, and that encourage superiors to talk about themselves. As we've mentioned in other chapters, people like to talk about their lives, their interests. Find chances to relate to them as humans rather than just bosses.

SEVEN TIPS FOR SUCCESSFUL INTERACTION WITH UPPER MANAGEMENT

Context and personality greatly determine appropriate interactions with superiors and bosses, so always be attuned to such factors. And keep these general guidelines in mind.

1. Don't always talk about business. This may seem counterintuitive but upper management talks business all day long. More business talk just becomes part of the blur. So when you run into them in the hall, at lunch, or at a business dinner, approach small talk on a personal level. They're likely to appreciate the "down time" and are likely to remember personal things about you. Theresa, a human resources manager for a large east coast mutual funds company for many years, puts it this way, "CEOs and vice presidents want to feel as comfortable in conversation as anyone else. Asking them about themselves, their family, or their golf game is conversationally relaxing. As busy as they are, casual contact is not something that they want to have to work at."

2. Follow upper management's lead. Taking tip #1 into consideration, if business is what they are obviously most comfortable talking about (to the exclusion of everything else), engage in business talk. Perhaps shift the conversation to business on a more general level. Show awareness about how a world event or emerging market may impact your business. This can help to take business talk in fresh directions.

3. Be upbeat. Bosses want to hear that you're onboard and they like brevity. After a meeting you might interject comments such as, "I'm optimistic about the new focus for the company" or "Great meeting. I think that the new sales strategies will net good results in my region."

4. Be in the moment. Every contact is a chance to make a good impression. Use your attention and body language to convey warmth and respect, and to show you're fully

present during quick or prolonged exchanges. Be especially vigilant about not yawning or looking at your watch (even if you're running off to a meeting). You don't want to send the message that they're keeping you from something more important.

5. Be authentic. As we've discussed, most people can detect phony behavior. Comments along the lines of: "I've really enjoyed my first few months with the company," or "I always wanted to play this golf course, thanks for making that possible," are acceptable to a boss. Just don't fawn. People in upper management may avail themselves of the energies of someone trying to suck up or curry favor, but they won't respect them.

6. Don't fake knowledge or feign interests you don't have. This can backfire. Why chance looking stupid? If you don't know the answer to a question, say you're not sure but will get back to them with an answer. Likewise, if you've never actually swung a golf club, don't pretend otherwise. You don't want to find yourself teamed up with the company president for a round of golf at the next sales meeting. Instead, try being curious about a subject you don't know much about.

7. Don't interrupt. Resist the temptation to jump in with a comment when other people are talking, especially with a superior who is probably used to having the floor. A well considered thought at an opportune moment is a much better strategy. Contribute meaningfully. Don't be the person who feels that they always have to make a comment in order to highlight their presence.

COWORKER FELLOWSHIP

Get to know your coworkers just as you would with a neighbor. Be curious and interested. Here you have the added benefit of seeing them nearly every day so there are opportunities galore for interaction and learning about each other. People get familiar with each other working side by side; they invite each other out for coffee or lunch. You may volunteer to join outside associations that support your work, making additional business contacts using your small talk savvy. There are natural avenues for being of assistance to one another, whether it's through research assistance, brainstorming, presentation preparation, or just providing a compassionate ear when other relationships or work projects aren't faring as well. Such opportunities reinforce your relationships and create a pleasant, mutually supportive work atmosphere.

Understand how people individually contribute to the workplace. Know who does what, without making assumptions about titles and work connections. Sue, a vice president at an investment firm, told this story of a hierarchy conjecture gone awry. A male coworker invited her to a networking gathering for both his current and former coworkers. Speaking with another man, she commented that she presently worked with Dave (the host). "Oh, are you his assistant?" the guy automatically responded, indicating his clear notions about male/female roles in the workplace. "No," she replied slowly, with a smile. "I'm his boss." Such assumptions (including age-related assumptions) can pretty much leave the conversation and the potential connection no place to go. If you do find yourself in the uncomfortable position of making a faux pas there are a couple of ways to make amends. Admit your error with sincere simplicity: "I apologize. I misspoke," or "I'm sorry for the mistake, it's been that kind of day." Some people find it easier to admit a mistake by using humility and humor: "I'm such an idiot sometimes. I hope you'll pardon my ignorance," "This is not going as well as I'd hoped, can we start over?" or "Maybe I should just stick to listening." Pick a strategy to change the energy of the exchange and then proceed without beating yourself up too much. It happens to everyone. How you handle it can actually work in your favor in some instances.

CLIENT MIXING

Clients have a social face and a business face. At any given time, they reflect diverse aspects of both their personal and professional personalities. Understand what it is they want from you and you succeed in being on the same wavelength in communication. The assumed boundaries in business can be very sterile; test these limits. Engaging clients on an emotional level may help you to build your relationships. Figure out the drill. Know when to be direct and when to be diplomatic. Know when to be cheerfully friendly and when to be work focused.

Successful interactions based on an understanding of the layers inherent in the business world require a basic understanding of the subtleties of communication. To know how your personality best works within any business atmosphere and what communications strategies are useful, be aware of standard business layers:

- Corporate/company personalities—Is the company traditional or cutting-edge, uptight or laid back? Any interviewee is smart to do their homework about a company prior to interviewing so they know what to expect, what's expected, and what type of personality succeeds in that environment. Likewise, new employees can get interactions off to a good start by observing interactions at the various levels: understanding interaction dynamics between secretaries/assistants and their bosses, between entry-level positions and middle management, between middle management and upper management. Who interacts well with all these levels, and who has an attitude? What is the dress code? Successfully meeting with a targeted potential client demands the same kind of research into corporate or company personality. Know thy work playmates.

- Individual personalities—The personalities of the people you work with have a big impact on your interactions. You meet all types of people, extroverts/introverts, go-getters/slackers, people who jump into a group dynamic with aplomb/people who are independent thinkers and workers. Get to know what people are like as individuals. Additionally, there are personal factors that you can't control, but which you might need to take into consideration. Is someone having a bad day? Fair or not, such life factors get brought into business meetings and into conversations. Sometimes, such "illogical" factors can make communications puzzle-like. Looking at an entire interaction, you have to decipher which reactions are a legitimate result of your input and which are not.

- Age differences—Someone twenty-four is going to have different life experiences than someone who is fifty-four. Take age into consideration when you interact. Be sensitive to age factors. Be respectful and understand what behavior and attitudes are appropriate to people of various ages.

You can probably plop down into the office of a twenty-something graphic artist, but may want to say "Excuse me, may I come in?" when you are talking to the fifty-year-old office manager.

- Gender differences—Gender differences may mean adjusting your interaction style. It's not unusual to find business books that use war and sports metaphors for business, as many men are comfortable with the "business is war" concept. Women are more apt to view business as personal, and about relationship building. Knowing the approach your coworkers and bosses take can enhance your communications.

The key to successful communication is judging your audience, and then showing an appreciation for people's differences in personality and stature. Some of the worst communication faux pas result from someone treating everyone the same: using the same jokes with coworkers, bosses, and clients; employing casual body language (i.e., feet on the desk) regardless of who is in the room or being addressed; projecting one "working" personality (super-serious/ambitious/ingratiating/relaxed) with all people. No person is all one thing and people instinctively know this, so such behavior rings false. Be yourself, while employing tactics that positively impact communication.

THE PERCEPTION CHECKUP

There are all kinds of formal tests designed to let you know how others perceive you and that categorize your general work personality. You may have taken one. These can be valuable because how we think we are seen and how we are actually perceived may be two different realities. For instance, the quietly efficient workers take it for granted that their hard work is being recognized and appreciated, and that by not going to the boss to "toot their own horn" they present one less time-consuming face for her to deal with. The perception by your superior: She never hears good news from you. She knows you are a good employee but you don't stand out from the crowd; exact details about project successes don't readily come to mind.

Don't make assumptions. Check in with coworkers and superiors every now and again. Directly ask about general perceptions of your work with coworkers whose opinion you value. At a minimum, ask your superior at review time. Ascertain their expectations for "reporting," and how they view your participation. Remember your achievements also reflect well on them. In many social situations you enter the game with a clean slate—there aren't preconceived ideas about how you behave or about who you are as a person. At work you build a positive or not-so-positive reputation over time. Keeping tabs on your work persona helps you to better access and plan beneficial mingling, networking, and interaction steps that will foster a desirable work image.

WORKPLACE ETHICS

Ethics in the workplace can refer to everything from a company paying its bills/vendors on time or refraining from malicious business dealings to being a company that adheres to its mission statement (walks the talk). Individually, the business world presents plenty of occasions for testing our personal ethical nature and our ability to adhere to positive rules for behavior and to resist the negative ethics of a given workplace. Small talk will not get you very far if you aren't someone people respect. Some general rules:

- No backstabbing.
- Do not engage in petty gossip.
- Show integrity/speak the truth.
- Give employees you manage the guidance and support they need to succeed.
- Respect differences/different work styles.
- Do the right thing/don't rationalize improper behavior (there are not as many gray areas in ethical behavior as people would like to convince themselves exist).
- Appropriately recognize personnel achievements.
- Give credit where credit is due.
- Don't create "fires" to put out.

EMULATE SUCCESS

So who's your work guru? Break it down. What exactly do you find admirable (besides their paycheck)?

- Ability to handle any situation
- Take-charge or never-say-die attitude
- Effective diplomatic manner
- Marketing and public relations expertise
- Negotiation or mediation skill
- Honesty and integrity
- Inventiveness/intelligence
- Facility for forecasting trends

- Thinking outside the box
- Dynamic personality
- Professional longevity
- Using success to help others
- Endless energy for their passion

Once you know what it is you admire, you can better decide if you have the right personal strengths necessary to emulate their particular brand of business acumen. If not, investigate what you could do to develop your business profile—take business courses or professional classes, network, join Toastmasters, and so on. Success in the workplace nearly always relies on success with relationships both in business and outside the workplace.

Interaction Strategies Outside the Office

Business outside the office has its own dynamic—part working personality and part social beast. It calls on us to maintain a professional demeanor while being engaging, to be wise while extending our personal selves. As is true for any social situation, interaction outside the office can take us outside the comfort zone we've developed at our place of business, whether that's a traditional office or a home office. Also, face-to-face encounters often include interacting with more than one individual at a time. The idea is for you to build communication skills that factor in aspects like thinking on your feet, spontaneity, manners, and connecting by using your mind, body, and spirit in harmony.

NETWORKING: INTRODUCTIONS AND CHATTING WITH FLAIR

You're probably a networking pro by now, with all the chitchatting you've been doing with your neighbors, and as a result of the focused attention you give each interaction. Business networking takes the basics of such exchanges a step further by adding an "active data" component. Typically, "active data" is information about a business product, service, or personal referral that may be of use to another person and vice versa, relevant data that another person makes available to you. It's not enough to meet a person, get their name, and find out about their personal life. You want to create a mutually beneficial connection that has the potential to positively affect business either in the here-and-now or down the road.

Business networking can be structured or unstructured. Some events are planned specifically for networking, and most business-related events inherently include an aspect of networking. It takes place at events such as monthly association meetings, specific group gatherings like Women in Business, chambers of commerce, volunteer organizations, trade show conferences, and civic meetings.

A SAFE RISK

Networking can be an intimidating process for those who get nervous or feel out of place around strangers. Yet, each new networking event is really a safe haven for making fresh connections. After all, no one has expectations about what you are like. There's no history or impressions established yet. Embrace this fact to create levity around professionally pursuing your networking goals. In addition, networking meetings are typically transitory—new people are regularly coming into the group, providing fresh contact potential. And, you can always go your separate ways if a contact does not flourish. As with personal day-to-day relationships, it's the nature of business networking to have hits and misses.

When you're feeling nervous as you enter a room of strangers, enter confidently, using your body language—standing tall and smiling—to ground you in the moment. Fight any urge to flee by considering that in a networking situation you have the advantage of knowing that people in attendance expect you to approach them, to be somewhat forward, and make the rounds. Furthermore, you come with gifts in hand—a service, product, or personal contacts that may be beneficial to others. In this context, what you do and whom you know, along with your likable personality, are key assets that people expect you to "sell."

THE ELEVATOR SPIEL

Prepare an elevator spiel for networking occasions. This is an explanation of who you are, what you do, your expertise or business philosophy, and any notable successes, brief enough in length to be shared on an elevator ride. An elevator spiel may sound like this: "My name is Sue Smith from San Diego. I'm an award-winning residential interior designer in business for ten years. I focus on contemporary design featuring environmentally friendly and sustainable building and interior materials." As you network, such a prepared description can be introduced into conversation naturally either all at once or as appropriate. At some networking meetings each person is asked to stand up and introduce himself. Be prepared and you will be at ease when the spotlight shines on you.

SMALL TALK FORAGING

One friend amusingly refers to networking as foraging behavior. You seek and find communication nourishment: some to be consumed immediately, additional data to be stockpiled for later use. Effective networking benefits from small talk that encourages the outpouring of tasty information. You have pretty wide latitude here as questions can combine both business and personal aspects. Taking a business stance you might ask:

- "I haven't seen you here before. Are you new to this networking group?"
- "Are you familiar with today's speaker? The topic sounds interesting."
- "Hi, nice to meet you, Joan. I'm new to this networking group. Can you tell me what you like most about this particular group?"
- "Debra, what type of clients typically use your financial counseling services?"

Likewise, you can be more personal:

- "Joan, you live in the area, can you recommend a good restaurant for lunch?"
- "Gary, I saw you drive up in a hybrid. How do you like it?"

One networking weakness is that people often form "comfort cliques" at regular networking events—talking and eating with the same people each month. It's ironic: People open themselves to risk-taking and new opportunity by networking in the first place, and then cling to the first comfort zone they can find. This inhibits real mixing and mingling, and often means no open spots at their table for new people.

Embark upon networking as equal parts business and social training. To be successful you need to be prepared and approachable, focused and engaging. You should walk away with tangible results—business cards to add to your Rolodex, contacts to follow up with, and perhaps products or services sold. Concentrate on interacting genuinely, exhibit self-confidence, be in the moment, listen attentively and show interest, ask both business and personal questions, offer helpful information as the opportunity arises, and have a sense of play about the encounters.

UNHELPFUL BUSINESS BEHAVIOR

Business activities such as meetings, network gatherings, association assemblies, and work retreats are ideal environments for establishing your reputation, conveying your business smarts, and for enlarging your realm of business contacts. Yet, these same happenings can be potential danger zones for poor communication behavior. The pressures of doing business, of occasionally finding oneself not adequately prepared, and wanting desperately to shine, can bring out less-than-helpful behavior. Not everyone finds that she is the personification of grace under pressure. So in addition to paying attention to helpful communication tips, it's important to know WHAT NOT TO DO as you interact.

- Don't be question crazy. Don't fire off questions in a nervous *ratatattat* and then not give the person you're addressing a chance to answer by continuing to ask more questions. Questions are not merely dead air filler; they should come from a real sense of interest. You want to learn; you want to discover points of commonality and mutually beneficial areas for support or assistance.

- Don't be a neurotic talker. Save free association and mono-logues for the acting class. Rambling about nothing very interesting, or conversing with no point in mind, will cause you to lose your listeners' attention. Try an engaging anec-dote related to the topic of conversation instead.
- Don't be a success monopolizer. Limit your recitations of all your accomplishments and winning business strategies to a reasonable length and encourage others to relate their strengths or business history. Especially avoid turning every topic of conversation into an opening for telling others how successful you are at that particular thing. If a topic comes up that naturally enables you to relate a pertinent story, by all means share it. Just don't brag to the extreme.
- Don't be a blank slate. Take ownership of what you've accomplished and communicate your enthusiasm for what you do.
- Don't be impolite. Nerves can create energy that is difficult to harness. If you are speaking with just one person, don't interrupt or call into question a comment being made. Try to wait until they have clearly stopped talking to add your thoughts or to considerately question someone. If you are networking with a group of people, politely interject without rushing or running over the thoughts of others. Be aware of how often you speak. If someone is more reticent than the other participants, draw them out with a direct question: "Susan, tell us something about your business."

- Don't be negative. A good impression stems from an upbeat presence as well as positive and encouraging words. Complaining, blaming, gossiping, or confronting make poor communication pals.

THE NAME GAME

Nearly everyone has, at some point, forgotten or been unable to recall a name, often at the most inopportune moment. These I-can't-believe-I-just-blanked-on-their-name instances are awkward on many levels. While you can't count on 100 percent recall, there are tricks that can help to bolster your name recall ability.

First, be fully present during that first encounter. Make sure you give the new person your full attention—without wandering mental chatter.

Secondly, lock eyes and repeat the person's name as you respond to the introduction: "Hi, Jake, so glad to meet you." As you talk continue to use their name, "Jake, when did you get into town for the convention?" "Jake, is this your first time to this networking group?" If you forget the name within the initial conversation, politely ask him to repeat it one more time. Generally, this is less stressful than to have to do it the next time you run into him.

Use your own interests to help with recall. If you know someone with the same name, silently reinforce this connection by saying to yourself, "Oh, Elizabeth like my cousin Elizabeth." Relate the name to someone famous or to a popular culture image if an association immediately comes to mind: Charlie as in *Charlie's Angels*, or Maria, like the *West Side Story* song. Some people lightheartedly voice the connection they are thinking of to the person they are meeting for the first time, "John Jones, any relation to Tom Jones?" This introduction tactic provides the other person with a chance to play off the connection you made.

Be creative. Some people employ rhymes to remember a name. Have fun with the rhyme so it is memorable. The rhyme may even include information about the person's profession: Sue, Sue the cosmetic guru, or Brad, Brad the restaurant comrade. You could associate the name with something the person is wearing: Heather, soft name, soft sweater. Associate the name with the person: Bob, short name, short guy; Angelina, angelic name, sweet person.

Create a definition for the name. For example, Jake Brown is a satisfactory (jake) earth color (brown); Diana is a Greek goddess; Lily is a flower. Also, you might better remember the name by categorizing it: Ty as in Ty Cobb, a sporty name; Joan as in Joan of Arc, a religious name. Associate the name with a specific ethnicity if that aspect of the name stands out: Colleen sounds Irish; or Margot sounds French.

Like other small talk tactics, name games become easier and more automatic with repeated use. At an initial meeting, it's most important to remember a first name, so concentrate on that if trying to recall a last name seems like too much, especially in a situation in which you are meeting many people.

Nametags provide a visual reinforcement along with the audio introduction. If you are the person initiating the contact at a networking or trade show and are looking at a nametag, take a mental picture of the name, including any other information on the nametag such as company name or location. Then say, "Hello Barbara, my name is Melissa. I see that you are from Boston." This reinforces the name and place connection and launches you into small talk such as, "Are you glad to be getting a break from the cold weather?" Some people like to covertly take in the information on a nametag, but there's nothing wrong with being obvious about it either. And, by being obvious, if any of the information is in error or the written name isn't their preferred moniker, the wearer is more likely to point it out. If a last name (or first) is difficult for you to pronounce simply give it a once-through and ask, "Did I pronounce that correctly?"

Forgetting a name is never optimal, but there are some strategies that can help you recover as gracefully as possible. If the face looks familiar, wait to see if talking with the person for a few minutes jars your memory. You may be able to get through the conversation without needing to verbalize their name, and can then find someone to tell you their name afterward. Sometimes it's best to simply limit your duress by admitting to your mental failing. "I'm sorry, this is a little distressing but I've forgotten your name," or "I'm embarrassed to admit that my memory isn't what it should be, could you please tell me your last name again?" Most people will understand, especially if you can recall something else about them: "I remember that you live in Philadelphia and have a teenage daughter, but I can't for the life of me recall your name." If you've forgotten a name and find yourself needing to introduce them to someone, introduce the person you know first and see if the mystery person will fill in their name. If they don't fill in the blank, you'll have to admit that their name escapes your recall: "I'd like to properly introduce you to my coworker Julie, but I'm having a bad memory day. Could you please tell me your name again?" As with all conversation, be warm and genuine and others are likely to forgive such a common lapse.

Take Note

If the introduction is an especially important connection, make notes after a conversation or an event that will help you to remember the particulars of a person. You will be able to use the information in conversation the next time you see them or when you follow up with a note or a phone call. People are generally flattered to have others recall facts about them.

TRADE SHOWS: POINTERS FOR YAKKING IN THE AISLES

What comes to mind when you think trade shows? Aching feet and an overabundance of stimuli? How about as one big happy business neighborhood? After all, a trade show is essentially a metropolis comprising of vendors, competitors, customers, window shoppers, amusements, and visitors. So approach it as you would a new town. That is, comfortably, with curiosity and a sincere desire to create connections. Make "dates" (appointments) in advance. Set a communication goal: Know whether you are interested in a few quality contacts or want to visit (meet) as many exhibitors as possible. Having a goal in mind enables you to be direct with the people you come in contact with about how they should interact with you: briefly and to the point, or fully engaged with more in-depth explanations. And know what you want to communicate to others, what personal and professional aspects are important to convey.

ATTENDEES: CLOSE AND CURIOUS ENCOUNTERS

From an attendee perspective, trade show conversations can tell you many different things about a company: its corporate personality, the company's standing/reputation within the industry, the general personality of a company's employees (are they dressed in business casual, conservatively in suits, or wearing matching clothing items such as vests or golf shirts?), the inventiveness of products, or the fresh take on a needed service. As an attendee, trade show smarts include employing opening lines and questions such as:

- "Hello, Joan, I understand that you are the expert on [fill in the blank as appropriate]."
- "Hi, Robert. I'm Mary Smith from company X. I'd like to take a look at your new products."
- "Sarah, this is my first year at this trade show and your booth caught my eye. How did you decide on this design concept for your exhibit?" (This should give you information about the company's marketing strategy and may be instructive about the company's personality. If the person doesn't know this information, you may infer that there is a serious lack of communication between departments.)
- "Hello, Matthew. This show is really busy for me and I'm on a tight schedule. Could you briefly point out the key points of your products/services that are most important for me to know?"

- "Wow, you've really generated some great traffic at your booth. Who had the clever idea to put on a dance revue?"
- "Emily, I like your booth, it's a real attention-getter. What can you tell me about your business?"
- "Hi, Zach, can you answer a few questions for me?"

EXHIBITORS: PUTTING COMMUNICATION SMARTS ON DISPLAY

If you are an exhibitor, you know that no single environment is more competitive than a trade show. You are competing for the very aspects that make human relations work: someone's attention, ear, interest, and desire to make a connection. You are probably familiar with the typical tactics companies and entrepreneurs employ to grab attention in order to show their products or to convey a business service: scantily clad showgirls, scantily clad models conducting prizewinning games, and autograph-signing athletes. Since many of us don't have access to such ploys, we develop our savvy about how to use our own creativity and personality to charm the masses, so to speak, by creating connection opportunities one person at a time. Consider the following sampling of trade show strategies.

1. DISARM THE PEOPLE

Stefan, president of an employee-screening firm, states that he relies on catching people's attention with the unexpected in order to maximize the advantages of the setting. "At most trade shows, so much out of the norm is going on that you can step out of a strictly traditional role and try tactics that you wouldn't in other business settings. Sometimes I will stop a person passing by our booth by handing them a company premium and saying with a straight face, 'You just cannot leave here without this, you'll need it to get on the plane.' It's disarming enough to make them pause and laugh or make a remark like 'Yeah, what makes this so special?' I get the opening I need to start talking business." As is true for social situations, keeping perspective and a sense of humor can work well in a trade show atmosphere, where socializing skills facilitate networking and can be conducive to conducting enjoyable business. What you don't want is to project desperation or the impression of being totally ill at ease in your surroundings. It's just not inviting and people will avoid entering such an atmosphere.

2. THE GIVEAWAY OPENER

Use communication strategies that feel comfortable to you, that are a good fit for your personality. If being disarming is a stretch, don't go there. Know your audience and focus on selecting giveaways that will entice the specific convention-goers you are targeting. Donna, a public relations expert based in New Jersey, used copies of the latest *Dilbert* book to entice a high-tech audience. Participants needed to sign up for a chance to obtain a copy—providing the perfect pause to begin small talk. "Thanks for stopping by, we're showing a new product that's almost as much fun as *Dilbert*." Well-chosen giveaways provide a perfect buffer for comfortably leading you into business small talk. Ideally, the giveaway should either tie in to a theme/product or service feature that you are conveying at the show, or should be so universally desirable to your audience that they will generate activity and get people talking.

3. STOP 'EM WITH VISUAL IMPACT

Can't hire the dancing bears? Try a visual that packs a punch. This could be a fabulous photograph with a catchy caption.

Declare product or service benefits boldly. Partner a poster with one of those "did you know" type statements that most people can't resist and you've created your opening line with strangers and potential customers who stop by your exhibit.

Tracy, a regional sales manager for a national company, confirms that visuals do catch his eye as he walks a convention floor and that they provide an easy way to begin a conversation. "The visual gets me to stop, to investigate the product or company. Then I ask questions like, 'How long have you been manufacturing this product?' or 'Has this been a good product for you?'" Likewise, Susan, a landscape architect with the National Park Service, stated that the most intriguing and alluring visuals catch her attention.

KEEP THEM SMALL TALKING

Once people come to your exhibit, be prepared to engage them in a meaningful way. If all you do is hand out freebies, without creating a personal connection or without exchanging information, you'll miss a great opportunity to get the word out and to generate leads that you can follow up afterward. Trade shows bring prospective customers right to you, so know what you want people to remember about your booth or business. Do you want to convey one central theme or are you trying to sell a specific product or concept? Do you want to broadcast benefits that address a pervasive industry issue or would you like to make clear that customer service is your forte? Pointing out useful information found in a brochure is a nonthreatening way to involve a potential customer in conversation. Remember, use open-ended questions; they are the most engaging and tend to elicit responses that naturally lead to your next question or comment. Try opening lines and questions like:

- "Hi, Madison, thanks for visiting us. Maybe you could share with me a little about what you are looking for?"
- "I'm glad you stopped by for the raffle, Nick. Now that I've got your attention, what do you think about our products?"
- "Ah, so our photograph caught your eye. What do like best about the image?"
- "Hi there. I see you're reviewing our service benefits. Which benefit surprises you?"
- "Thanks for making the time to stop by. Tell me something about your business needs."
- "Hi, Rebecca. So what are you seeing at the show today that's making an impression?"
- "Hello, Ethan. What questions can I answer for you?"
- "Emma, you look like the kind of person whose opinion I would respect. We're trying to get a sense about how people feel about . . . " (an industry issue, the impact of a news event on consumer buying behavior, a certain product or service feature, etc.).
- "Ryan, it's nice to see you again. What do you think about the booth this year?"

Make your brief exchange count. Take the lead if you aren't approached directly. Capture initial interest with pleasant conversation. Push your comfort boundaries while staying upbeat. And, don't exert too much pressure on the participant to respond in a particular manner that fills some invisible quota. Add to that winning formula visual stimulation, some giveaway enticements, and the distribution and exchange of useful information, and trade shows don't have to be a painful series of rejections, blank stares, and fumbling conversations.

One other thought on showing your communication savvy. Trade shows typically offer topic-specific sessions that present opportunities for networking and making good impressions upon associates and people in your industry. If you know in advance that there will be an open discussion or that participants will be encouraged to ask questions of a panel of experts, be prepared to ask a question in the most intellectual way you can. Susan, the landscape architect, recommends: "If I'd like the answer to a specific question, or want to take the discussion in a particular direction or open it up to a controversial topic, I come prepared with a question I want to articulate well and in a polite and respectful manner. What you don't want to come off as is pedantic or to discredit yourself in front of business peers."

The Small Talk Handbook skills help to organize communication efforts in a way that facilitates successful business contacts and enhanced satisfaction with personal participation. Tactics like forethought and planning, physical presentation, an optimistic and confident attitude, a sincere smile and warm handshake, genuine interest and enthusiasm, a sense of humor, and telling personal stories that make you memorable boost your success rate.

CHAPTER 9

Taking Stock of Your Small Talk Skills

Finally, just about all that needs to be said about small talk has been articulated. Now you are ready to put yourself out in the world and mingle among the people. Be kind to yourself and persevere. Don't let lingering fears or frustration manifest as disinterest, ennui, or as anger at others or yourself. Growth always has its awkward moments and proceeds in increments, often more slowly than we'd like. Be patient with yourself and watch for the small and significant advances.

- An evolving attitude about socializing (i.e., from hating it to nervous trial and error, from self-conscious participation to eagerly searching out social opportunities)
- Gradually feeling more comfortable in your own skin, and more forgiving of occasional flubs
- Body language awareness tuning you into others' attitudes and reactions
- Increased confidence in new situations
- A playful manner activating instances of lighthearted banter
- An expanding personal world as a result of adding informational texture and color to daily life
- "Aha" moments of understanding when conversation tactics work
- Dialogue skills boosting the enjoyment quotient of dating
- Social risk-taking and spontaneity increasing/enhancing your social network
- Improved communication savvy at work resulting in an enhanced business image

Over time, the potential for personal growth is huge! And, with time being the swift flier that it is, before long you'll feel yourself on a small talk par with the rest of the world. How much fun is that?

THE SOCIAL MIND SELF-ASSESSMENT

All action stems from a particular attitude, a certain mindset that is part of our personality at any given time. We can change the results we get by altering our expectations and our focus. Let's see where you are today. Answer Yes or No to the following statements.

1. My attitude about making new connections is generally positive.
2. I'm less blasé or negative about going out socially.
3. I am in charge of my self-confidence.
4. I can anticipate a time when small talk will be a "no-brainer."
5. I honestly believe that a sense of levity will help me in small talk.
6. I plan to work on projecting a positive presence.
7. It's okay to be nervous; it's good energy I can use.
8. Diversifying and enhancing my interests will be fun.
9. Social ease is equal parts exposure, expenditure, and experience.
10. I'm more interested in face-to-face encounters than electronic relationships.
11. I've taken stock of my strengths and personal assets.
12. Already, I'm more observant of others and my surroundings.
13. I'm trying to be more spontaneous.
14. My listening skills have improved.
15. I can name two body language cues that help others know that I am interested in them.
16. I'm trying not to predetermine the results of my social interactions.
17. I believe that the (learning) process is as important as the result.

18. I've pinpointed specific areas where I can make small talk advances (attitude, conversational style, better listening, personal revelation, eye contact, having topics in mind, etc.).

19. I have the lead role in determining my relationship successes.

20. I've tried some of the small talk prompts.

If you answered 1–5 yes: Either you don't believe everything you read or you're not sure you have what it takes to overcome your social weaknesses. Try anyway. Let action stand in for confidence for a while. Focus on one area of your life that could benefit from enhanced social skills. Try some of the suggested exercises consistently for two or three months.

If you answered 6–10 yes: The spirit is willing but the mind has a few lingering doubts and, perhaps, the body hasn't quite kicked into high gear. As you try the tactics, paying attention to tips for building positive communication skills (as well as ineffective behavior), your emotional, mental, and physical sides should start to harmonize. Take one step at a time and keep progressing. As needed, refer back to the book to refresh yourself on specific strategies. This is a work in progress.

If you answered 11–15 yes: You have the right attitude. Now all you need are new experiences and a track record of small successes in order to gently persuade yourself that you're fully in charge of this portion of your life. It only gets better from here on out.

If you answered 16–20 yes: You're absolutely ready to be a small talk pro! Your commitment to making this work for an enhanced social experience should help make the process enjoyable.

BUILDING SMALL TALK ASSETS

As we've discussed, no person is one thing all the time (whether it's shy or outgoing, unsure or confident), and no one person is defined by one personality trait. Just as some days we're more moody or energetic, there are times when we just feel more social. Fortunately, we have each new day in front of us to try something new, to change an attitude or action that's not working. Concentrate on building small talk assets rather than trying to dismantle perceived negative aspects of one's self. Positive actions will create positive reactions in your life. Take the following True/False quiz to further measure your small talk know-how.

SMALL TALK KNOW-HOW: TRUE-OR-FALSE QUIZ

1. If I don't make a positive first impression the relationship potential is doomed.
2. The best assets to bring to a social event are a sense of humor, self-confidence, and realistic expectations.
3. It's better to lie if you're not interesting.
4. Only shy people get nervous in the public eye.
5. The Four Ps of dating are: plan, parade, persevere, and pop the question.
6. An open-ended question means that the person can choose whether or not to answer you.
7. A smile is a great tool for deception.
8. If I act busy people will think that I have an interesting life.

9. At-home entertaining and business meals are a wonderful way to nourish relationships.

10. In business, good topics of conversation include the weather, current events, industry news, family, and humorous personal stories.

ANSWERS

1. False. Yes, first impressions are ideal, but small talk skills such as self-deprecating humor, body awareness, a warm smile, and "interested" questions can get most anyone past a few awkward first moments.

2. True. There are many personal assets you can "bring to the party," but this dynamic trio especially ensures that your social interactions will flow naturally and be enjoyable.

3. False. Lying is inauthentic. It's better to use your energy to actually be interesting than to waste energy covering for false information.

4. False. Nearly everyone has moments of nervousness. The key is to reduce nervousness with planning and enhanced communication skills, as well as to translate nervousness into an uplifting energy during interchanges.

5. False. The Four Ps of dating are: plan, primp, project, and promote.

6. False. An open-ended question requires more than a yes or no answer, helping to fuel conversation and elicit meaningful answers.

7. False. A smile is a great social skill to put others at ease, but it must be genuine or it will come across as a "fake front."

8. False. People are more likely to think that you overextend yourself or to feel that you don't have room in your life for

new friends and activities. Neither is conducive to growing your social or work contacts.

9. True. Making people feel welcome reflects positively on you—making new acquaintances feel good about being included and reinforcing friendships. Business-related meals tend to make people more relaxed and open, setting the stage for conversation and relationship building.

10. True. Many of the same topics used in social situations can be used in business, in addition to work related topics.

THE CELEBRATION CHECKLIST

Remember, people who truly enjoy connecting with other people tend to have a wider connection to the banquet of life offerings. Consciously or unconsciously, they use many of the tactics discussed in *The Small Talk Handbook*. Be open to new experiences. Find the fun in small talk. As you experiment with small talk strategies and have successes, keep track of them. Here is a checklist of successes that may be celebrated.

- ☐ I opened myself up to two new social opportunities this month (a new club, a neighborhood art walk, book club, etc.).
- ☐ Friends commented on me being more outgoing.
- ☐ My discomfort level when meeting new people has lessened.
- ☐ I used two "did you know" questions today.
- ☐ I had a conversation with someone completely different from me (in terms of looks, intellectual pursuits, lifestyle, etc.).

☐ I interviewed myself prior to an important social event.

☐ I'm consciously trying to be a good listener.

☐ I initiated a conversation that resulted in a date/a new friend.

☐ I'm cultivating curiosity about others and the world.

☐ I'm better at verbalizing compliments to others rather than just thinking them.

☐ I've gotten to know two people in my neighborhood.

☐ I hosted a dinner party, cocktail party, themed party, or holiday get-together.

☐ I made a point of talking with my _____ [Fill in the blank: mail carrier/post office clerk, grocery clerk, restaurant waiter/owner/chef, tailor/dry cleaner, coffee shop patrons, etc.].

☐ I made the first move to speak to someone new/to extend an invitation.

☐ I've explored retail stores in my town, introducing myself to the people working there.

☐ I extended spontaneous invitations to neighbors or coworkers for [circle appropriate activity] coffee, breakfast, lunch, a glass of wine, a leisure activity.

☐ I regularly go where people gather.

☐ I joined a professional association or networking group.

☐ I used a name game successfully.

☐ I've participated in a charity group function, spiritual related group activity, arts or entertainment organization event, alumni group activity, sporting team activity (softball game, bike club ride), cultural organization event, etc.

☐ I'm enriching my life with a class or how-to seminar, etc.

☐ I accepted an invitation I would have turned down last year.

☐ My boss complimented me on my new proactive participation.

☐ I'm getting to know my coworkers better.

☐ I did a better job connecting and following up with people I met at a work event.

☐ I prepared an introduction for myself that adequately reflects my accomplishments.

☐ I was a personable/outgoing person today.

These are just a few of the many accomplishments that should add up as you refine your small talk capabilities. As you practice projecting a cheerful and inviting attitude, and use body language to radiate ease and confidence, you will find all the components of effective interchange becoming more automatic.

KEEPING TRACK OF SMALL TALK SPECIFICS

Make a point of recalling what goes right for you in social and business encounters. Keep a notebook or journal that tracks some of the finer points of conversation. It not only reinforces success, it also helps you to better recall what doesn't work. Social entries might include the following:

- Most successful/least successful opening lines to date
- Interesting topics discussed
- Well-received jokes/jokes that fell flat
- "In the news" or entertainment information brought up successfully

- Situations in which self-deprecating humor was useful
- Insightful replies to questions
- Insights you've gleaned about yourself
- Good questions asked by other people
- Body language cues/mannerisms observed in others (and in what particular situations)
- Favorite place(s) to meet new people
- Small talk skills you've noticed other people use
- Topics you'd like to learn more about
- Actions that still feel unnatural
- Traits of good communicators/speakers

Remember, no one gets business interaction right all the time. Even super-confident, self-proclaimed business "smarties" make basic communication errors. Awareness and common sense, being genuine and checking in with others, speaking and acting with integrity, and engaging others in a timely and helpful manner are key to effective workplace communication. It's vital to your progress to be aware of and note what communication successes you experience related to work. Suggested business related developments to track:

- Progress you perceive in any specific business area (easier interactions with superiors, helpful actions in regards to coworkers, more confidence in meetings, successful mediation of a challenging work situation, strengthening of a client relationship, etc.)
- Comments made by others that indicate they perceive a positive difference (note in what area: general performance, communication effectiveness, approachability, friendliness, proactive participation, etc.)

- Wider circle of positive coworker connections
- New business-related newsletters or professional journals you are reading
- A communication skill you learned from being observant of someone else
- Beneficial networking connections
- Work insights or education (or certification) received from taking a course or class
- Letters, memos, or verbal input from clients commending attentive and/or effective interactions
- Proactive behavior that resulted in a positive outcome for self or company

Not only is this information supportive of your progress and good for building your self-confidence, it can also be used for things like self-evaluations that many companies request prior to review time, and in promotion or interview conversations.

THE OUTCOME OF ALL THIS BLATHERING

In the end, the result you desire from acquiring small talk confidence should be simple: you want to feel good about yourself and your interaction with others. You achieve this by following through on your intention to meet people, by resolving to be yourself, and to have a good time.

Over time, one new connection at a time, small talk improvements should inspire progressive and powerful thoughts like: "New situations stimulate me in a good way," "I enjoy being engaged with the world outside my job/home/current social circle," "I'm feeling more cheerful than nervous," and "I'm an interesting person." You may even notice that people are letting you know in various ways that you are having a positive impact on their lives. And, that is truly the mark of success for any relationship. So keep small talking!

Conversation Cheat Sheets

Conversation dynamics can be simplified by remembering that certain attitudes and actions are conducive to positive exchanges:

1. Exhibit genuine curiosity about people and an interest in connecting with them
2. Breathe: to stay in the moment and relax
3. Smile: the warm energy of a smile is contagious
4. Inject levity: don't take yourself too seriously and show a sense of humor
5. Listen well: to show respect and to learn
6. Engage others: get people to talk about themselves
7. Play off environmental stimuli: conversation topics lie in furniture, design, people, specific actions, clothes, food, wine, and so on
8. Display empathy and understanding: let people know you relate and/or hear their point of view
9. Show self: indicate commonalities as well as share your history and your interests
10. Be giving: offer helpful advice or information, and be responsible for contributing your share to conversation success

Small Talk Conversation Starters

Sometimes the best intentions go awry if it just seems like too much work. These lists are designed to help you get your conversations rolling.

CONVERSATION PROMPTS

Keep your small talk simple and keep it real. Try any of the following lines and questions (listed in no particular order) as appropriate, and at your discretion. Some are surface starter lines, while others are good probing questions that you can use as you get further along in conversation or a relationship. Remember: Use your observation skills, sense of curiosity, and specific knowledge to stimulate small talk.

- "It's such a beautiful day. Aren't you glad to be out enjoying it?"
- "What are you reading?"
- "What movies have you seen lately?"
- "What's your favorite food?"
- "What kind of music do you enjoy?"
- "What traits do you most admire in men/women?"
- "What's on your list to do before you die?"
- "Is there a talent that you wish you had?"
- "What are some of your favorite movies?"
- "What has been your proudest moment?"
- "From what I know, I think that the _____ [Renaissance, American colonial era, etc.] would have been an interesting time to be alive. In what period of history would you have liked to have been alive?"
- "Who do you think had a really great (or well-lived) life?"
- "I can't wait for spring. What's your favorite time of year?"
- "I just read about a _____ [fill in the description]. What is your favorite invention or gadget?"
- "What do you like to do in your downtime?"
- "What kind of work do you do? Do you enjoy it?"

- "What's your dream job?"
- "Do you go to hear speakers very often?"
- "Isn't this a nice party?"
- "It was so thoughtful of _____ [fill in the name] to organize this event. I'm really enjoying it."
- "If you could live somewhere else, where would you live?"
- "Name some adjectives that you think best describe you."
- "Who in your life is most important to you?"
- "Do you have a hero?"
- "Do tell . . . what's your most embarrassing moment?"
- "I think that you have the right idea. Mind if I join you?" (to someone sitting at a park bench, on a bench at the museum, etc.)
- "Do you have the time?"
- "Great hairstyle. Where do you go to get it done?"
- "You had a little rush there. Is it always so busy?" (to a shop owner/employee)
- "I love your store. Where do you find such beautiful things?"
- "Where did you grow up?"
- "What is your idea of bliss?"
- "What would you do with a million dollars?"
- "I overheard your interesting conversation. It made me think of . . . " or "I think that you're right . . . " or "Is that true?" (Good prompt for those times you are in line, waiting at a doctor's office, sitting next to people at a social or entertainment event, etc. If you find what others have to say of interest, decide whether it is appropriate to join in on the conversation.)
- "This weather is gloomy. How do you cope with all the rain?"

- "Beautiful dog. What is the breed?"
- "I've never bought loose tea before. Could you explain the differences in your green teas?"
- "I've been watching you and am fascinated. What are you doing? It looks interesting."

FAVORABLE CONVERSATION STARTER TOPICS

- Food
- Hobbies
- Films
- Books
- Sports
- Travel
- Interesting magazines/articles
- Current news
- What's "hot" or "in"

CONVERSATION STARTERS BEST SAVED FOR CLOSE FRIENDS AND MATES

- Politics
- Religion
- Medical problems
- Marriage/relationship concerns
- Child problems

Index

Assets, small talk, 139–41

Attitudes, 46

Behavior, self-protective, 17–18

Body language, 27–44

    arms/legs and, 37–38, 40

    awareness of, 28

    basic pointers on, 29–35

    communication and, 27, 28,
        30, 33

    dating and, 66

    direct eye contact and, 29–31

    face level and, 29

    formula for, 27

    lips and, 32

    mirroring and, 33, 43–44

    neck/head and, 32–33

    negative/positive mental
        visuals and, 42

    poetic praise for, 40

    posture/poses and, 40–41

    smiling and, 31–32

    socializing and, 53

    temperament and, 28

    threatening/nonthreatening
        touching and, 36–37

    universal signals and, 28

    use of hands and, 35–37

    vocal cues and, 33–35

    work situations and, 36

Celebration checklist, 141–43

Chatterer, easy, 50–51

Communication

    body language and, 27, 28,
        30, 33

    competence, 15

    dynamics, 66–68

    effective workplace and, 144

    hands and, 35

    interaction strategies and,
        122, 123, 128, 129, 130, 131

    nonverbal, 32

    vocal cues and, 34

Communication—*continued*
workplace small talk
and, 108–09, 113, 115
Communication roadblocks,
78–88
commonalities/differences
and, 87–88
community standoffish
personalities and, 83–85
electronic junkies and, 79–81
living independent minded
and, 85–87
work overload and, 81–83
Community neighbors, 77–90
acting on interests and, 82
being complimentary
and, 87–88
being welcoming and, 88
common hindrances and, 78
connecting with style
and, 84–85
gifting with good presence
and, 83
interactions/observations
and, 81
inviting interaction and, 86
modern communications
quiz, 79–81

places for conversations
and, 88–90
smiling and, 81
social skill building exercises
and, 84–85
sparking connections and, 85
stimulating annual events
and, 87
Connections, network of, 17
Conversation
cheat sheets, 147
prompts, 150–52
quiz, 48–51
style, 46

Dating, 13, 61–75
appearances/impressions
and, 63–64
body language and, 66
communication dynamics
and, 66–68
developing interests/topics
for, 68–70
dos/don'ts, 72–75
mirroring and, 66
pitfalls and, 62
planning and, 63
projecting and, 64–65

question companion for, 71

sharing information and, 68

successful, 63–65

talking, listening, responding
    and, 66–68

Dinner parties/luncheons, 92

Dress codes/accessories, 52

Entertaining, home/business,
    91–103

after event follow-up and, 101

dinner parties and, 92

empathy/compassion and,
    102

energy/entertainment
    and, 96–98

etiquette/manners
    and, 99

host/hostess gifts and, 95

introductions and, 94

the invitation and, 93–94

levity/humor and, 102

the meal and, 98–100

party icebreakers and, 98

personal assets and, 102–03

seating arrangements
    and, 98–99

small talk topics, 95–96

volunteering assistance
    and, 95

Factors, uncontrollable, 18

First impressions, 57–59

How to Use Body Language
    (Livingston), 28

Interaction strategies, 119–34. *See
    also* Trade shows

active data and, 120

comfort zone and, 122

communication and, 122, 123,
    128, 129, 130, 131

elevator spiel and, 121

foraging behavior and,
    122–23

name recall abilities and,
    125–28

networking and, 120–23

safe risk and, 120–21

unhelpful business behaviors
    and, 123–25

Jonson, Ben, 40

Journaling, 143–45

Listener, 51
Livingston, Glenn, 28

Mehrabian, Albert, 27
Muscles, developing small talk, 19

Networking, 120–23
Nonverbal communication. *See* Body language

Observations, negative vs. positive, 23–25

Performer, 50
Personal revelations, 47
Physical presence, 46
Play, sense of, 25–26
Preparedness, 12

Questions, self-review, 20–22

Responsiveness, 47

Self-assessment, 136–39
Self-confidence, sense of, 18–22
Shakespeare, William, 40
Shyness, 13
Situations, unknowable, 18

Small talk, description of, 16–18
Social butterflies, 16
Social ease, 15
Social interaction, 13
Socializing, 45–59
    attitudes and, 46, 54
    awareness and, 53
    body language and, 53
    comfort point and, 58
    contact points and, 53–54
    conversation starters and, 54
    conversation style and, 46
    conversation style quiz and, 48–51
    dealing with strangers and, 58
    dress codes/accessories and, 52
    evaluating social skills and, 46–48
    first impressions and, 57–59
    mingling and, 54–55
    new social situations and, 58
    personal revelations and, 47
    physical presence and, 46
    pitfalls to avoid and, 55–56
    points of successful, 52–56
    responsiveness and, 47

seasonal dinner parties and, 92

walk away perception and, 56

Social situations, 25–26

Social skill building exercises, 81, 82–83, 84–85, 86–88

Social skills, evaluating, 46–48

Stern, John, 31

Sterne, Laurence, 40

Strengths, know your, 20

Survival accessories, 18–23

Tension, 18

Trade shows, 128–34

attendees/conversations and, 129–30

communication effectiveness and, 130–32

disarming people and, 130–31

engaging attendees and, 132–34

exhibitors and, 130–32

giveaways and, 131

topic-specific sessions and, 134

visual impacts and, 131–32

Traits, negative vs. positive, 22–23

Workplace small talk, 105–18

admiration and, 117–18

age differences and, 114–15

boss contact and, 108–11

client interactions and, 113–15

communication and, 108–09, 113, 115

corporation/company personalities and, 113–14

coworker fellowship and, 112–13

ethics and, 116–17

gender differences and, 115

implementing, 106

individual personalities and, 114

multistratum socializing/ mingling and, 108

perception and, 115–16

proper dress code for, 107

upper management interaction guidelines and, 109–11

About the Author

Melissa Wadsworth is an author, public relations professional, photographer, and artist. A self-professed introvert, she honed her small talk skills as a public relations specialist for nearly twenty years, becoming a vice president at thirty-three. In 1995, she started Wadsworth Communications, a media relations and marketing communications company with national clients throughout the United States. She lives in Seattle with her husband.